RICHARD A. SINGER JR

Eastern Wisdom for Your Soul

Anne,

Thank you so much for

Being you.

RICHARD A. SINGER JR

Eastern Wisdom for Your Soul

111 Meditations for Everyday Enlightenment

Dreamriver Press

Dreamriver Press LLC
www.dreamriverpress.com
or contact at:
12 Franklin Avenue
Flourtown, PA 19031-2006
U.S.A

First **Dreamriver Press** edition, 2007

ISBN-13:   978-0-9797908-0-5
ISBN-10:   0-9797908-0-8

Library of Congress Control Number:
2007932440

Designed by George D. Matthiopoulos

Printed and bound in The United States of America

This book is dedicated
to those seeking truth
and awareness
in their daily lives.

Please, never give up
on this precious journey.

Richard A. Singer is an award winning author, trained psychotherapist, and most importantly a seeker of truth. He continuously searches for wisdom to use in his life, as well as helping other human beings in their precious journey. He has studied eastern psychology, buddhist healing, and non-violence at the doctoral level; in addition, he has spent years devoted to the study of wisdom recorded throughout history. He seeks to impart this knowledge to the world through his writing. His primary purpose is to benefit humanity in any way possible. Richard states that "My books are not only for reading, they are meant to be lived."

Richard resides in the Cayman Islands with his wife Debbie and his twin sons, Matthew and Alexander.

Learn more about Richard A. Singer on his website www.YourDailyWalk.org and contact him at RAS9999@aol.com

CONTENTS

"Richard Singer has outdone himself! If you thought his first book, *Your Daily Walk with the Great Minds* was wonderful, you haven't read anything yet. Singer has taken the word 'mindfulness' to a new level and shows us how to apply it to every moment of our lives. A Japanese proverb says, "Beginning is easy, continuing is hard." However, they obviously hadn't read Singer's new book, *Eastern Wisdom for Your Soul: 111 Meditations for Everyday Enlightenment* — Richard has made it easy to begin and continue.

Sue Vogan,
author/radio show host

"I would highly recommend *Eastern Wisdom for Your Soul* to those seeking truth in life."

David J. Powell,
Ph.D., President International
Center for Health Concerns, Inc.
and Institute of Mental Health,
Beijing Medical University,
Beijing China

FOREWORD

It is my pleasure to introduce you to Richard's book of Eastern wisdom with its wise and wonderful quotes, commentary and exercises encapsulating millennia of spiritual truth. Repetition is the real source of power in self-development, and being reminded of good, wise thoughts by great spiritual leaders is a sure fire way of growing in wisdom and personal power.

I have done my own research into the great spiritual traditions, and was struck by the similarity of the themes in this book to what I have also learned. These themes include:

Acknowledgment of an unseen order

You do not have to believe in a religious 'God' to acknowledge that there is an invisible order to life which cannot be escaped. We can either get more in tune with this order, or resist it to our disadvantage. As the Old Testament prosaically puts it, "Many are the plans in a man's heart, but it is the Lord's purpose that prevails."

In Taoism this order is known as the Tao. It refers to the real nature of things, the force that governs the universe. In Hinduism it is expressed as karma and dharma. Whatever you call it, a life lived out of tune with the unseen order is a blind, frustrating life.

Divining of a life purpose

The great Swiss psychologist Carl Jung said that when a person enters the world, they represent a question mark. In how they live their life comes the answer. If you believe that we are 'spiritual beings having a human experience', as Teilhard de Chardin expressed it, then it follows you must also believe that we were created for a purpose.

A major element of spiritual practice must therefore be to divine the larger purpose of our lives, intuiting how we can increase the sum of knowledge and love in the world by using our talents and personality to the fullest extent. Instead of being an ego that strives to achieve its wants and desires, we can become a vehicle that makes good things happen. Being human, we of course fear the loss of the ego for greater ends, yet only in doing this will we achieve real peace and become truly powerful.

Letting go of the little self

We sometimes think that the greatest joy in life is to satisfy our bodily pleasures, but in doing so we miss the even greater satisfaction to be gained from leaving behind efforts to please the self.

The purpose of self-development is paradoxical, allowing us to go beyond the concerns and grasping of the ego, to take us beyond the self. We were not made for ourselves, said Al Ghazzali, the great Islamic scholar and mystic, we were made for God—it follows, then, that our greatest delight must lie in increasing our knowledge of the divine. A by-product of this is that such increased knowledge brings greater clarity about who we are and what our purpose in life may be.

Being present-minded
A king once looked far and wide to answer three questions: what is the best time to do each thing? Who are the most important people to work with? What is the most important thing to do at all times? When he received his answers, they were not at all what he expected: the best time is now, the most important people are the ones you are with, and the most important act is to make those people happy.

We all make the mistake of living for some imagined future instead of enjoying the treasures of the moment, but actually appreciating the 'miracle of mindfulness' is something so easy to forget to do. We should keep in mind what the main character in Dan Millman's classic, *The Way of the Peaceful Warrior*, learned from his mentor:

There are no ordinary moments!

Seeing the oneness of the universe

We humans like to notice opposites such as good and evil, praise and criticism and happiness and sadness. This is called 'duality'. But as all the great sages and saints have found, the nature of the universe is non-dualistic. That is, everything is One, and part of an essential indivisible beingness.

What is a person? As many of the quotes in this book will show, we are in reality splinters of consciousness from a much larger Mind. It is we that maintain the illusion of separateness, but through meditation and spiritual exercises we can shake off our individual mindsets and re-experience the Universal Mind. In doing so, we find the greatest freedom and equanimity.

I would like to add one more quote to Richard's great collection. It is a Persian proverb which reminds us of the real source of spiritual wisdom:

See truth in meditation, not in moldy books.
Look in the sky to find the moon, not in the pond.

What others have said is a wonderful way of getting us to look into the pond, but we must move our eyes up from its reflections to the sky itself. In meditation we can feel, understand and align ourselves with the 'unseen order' that guides the universe.

TOM BUTLER-BOWDON
Author

INTRODUCTION

This book has been written for one purpose: to help other human beings gain the peace and tranquility that I have received by applying the enlightened wisdom of the East to my own daily life. My personal interest and curiosity in Eastern wisdom started upon entering into addiction-recovery quite a few years ago.

What attracted me to the thinking of the East was its immense difference from the western religions I knew. In my view Eastern wisdom is a system of thinking or philosophy rather than a structured religion filled with dogma. Eastern thought in general, which is comprised of a variety of different philosophies, including Hinduism, Buddhism, Taoism, does not consist of strict boundaries, rigidity or exclusivity. The wisdom of the East offers freedom and is all inclusive in its approach

Although I personally do not practice a structured religion, I do consider myself to be a very spiritual person, having integrated into my life many principles of Eastern philosophies. It should, however, be clarified from the beginning that I do not consider myself a Guru, Sage, or an enlightened master. Nor am I an expert or scholar in the area of Eastern history, philosophy or religion, although some formal education in the area of Eastern thought, as well as extensive informal education through the personal study of these philosophies, have proven extremely helpful and enlightening over the years. The wisdom of the East contains Universal truths that have the capacity to transform each human being that practices them, as well as humanity as a whole.

As a result, this book is not based on any specific system of thought and is not meant to be religious in nature. Instead, it is simply a compilation of diverse teachings offered to you as a sample of the powerful and transforming wisdom of the East. It is meant to be practical in its use and not exhaustive in its content. Many books are read and then discarded shortly after. I do not believe this to be the purpose of a book, so what was created is practical – overflowing with wisdom – and easily applied to daily life. The wisdom in this book is eternal and should be used throughout your lifetime. If you do apply it to your life, you will develop and evolve further than you have ever imagined. You are not required to be a Buddhist, Taoist, or Hindu to benefit from these philosophies. The only requirements are that you keep an open mind and that you sincerely contemplate and internalize the words of this book.

Below is a quote by Shunryu Suzuki Roshi that I apply to my life on a daily basis.

If your mind is empty, it is always ready for anything;
it is open to everything. In the beginner's mind
there are many possibilities;
in the expert's mind there are few.

This precious and sacred information is brought to you from a beginner, and I hope you learn to apply the approach of starting over as a beginner to all aspects of your life too.

R.A.S.

ACKNOWLEDGEMENTS

I must acknowledge the great teachers in my life that have pushed me to seek the truth and explore the mysteries of the Universe. Each individual that I come in contact with on a daily basis offers an opportunity to teach me something significant about life, if I am open to the lesson. However, the teachers that I am referring to are those that indirectly forced me to look within myself and learn some of the greatest lessons of my life. Kahlil Gibran articulated these learning experiences quite eloquently when he said, "I have learned silence from the talkative, tolerance from the intolerant, and kindness from the unkind. I shall not be ungrateful for those teachers."

So I am now expressing my gratitude for these great teachers in my life. I would like to mention a few by name: Nick Collangelo, Jim Dougherty, Leigh Fierman, and Dominic Vangarelli. Also, Donald Potkins and Judith Seymour (without their indirect help I would have never written my first book), and Graham Walker and Tyra Miller (without their help I would not have been able to stay at home and raise my kids for the first months of their life or had the precious time to write this book). Thank you and I hope you learned as much from me as I have from you.

In addition, I must acknowledge the incredible mentors that have taught me priceless skills and have provided me with wisdom to use on my journey. They are: Michael Donahue, Dick Conaboy, Jim Debello, and Rob Olinits.

Finally, I must honor my precious family who provides unconditional love and teaches me about the value of life on a daily basis. They have also provided endless support and encouragement for this project, as well as everything else I choose to pursue in my life. These include my mother, father, step-father, sister, grandmother, wife, and the newest additions, our twins Matthew and Alexander, who have taught me more than I could ever imagine in their short lives thus far. I cannot express in words what all of you mean to me. Thank you for being there for me, now and always.

Let me not forget the two wonderful women who transformed my faulty writing into as close to perfection as possible. Editing was done by Sandra A. Willis and Helen Thomas. Thank you for your keen eye for perfection.

ORGANIZATION OF THE BOOK

I have divided up the 111 meditations in this book into 11 distinct sections; each of which briefly discusses a specific principle, followed by ten meditations to apply along your path to awareness and peace. My goal is to introduce you to each principle without excessive use of jargon or intellectualization, and provide you with the practical steps needed to apply this wisdom to your life. My writing style is simple; it comes directly from my heart and soul, and I try to leave out the intellectualization and analytical aspects driven by my ego. I genuinely believe in the words of Huang-Po, "Those who seek the truth by means of intellect and learning only get further and further away from it."

Each page contains a quote to ponder on, a short meditation to contemplate, allowing it to seep into the depths of your being, and a real life application of the meditation. You may find the meditations in each section repetitive, but I believe such repetition is necessary if you are to internalize these transformative principles and implement them in your life. Finally, I have included a creation of my own which discusses the popular Twelve Steps of Recovery in Eastern terms.

You can read through this volume and say, "That was wonderful information," or you can immerse yourself in the transformative power of this wisdom, and begin to live a life of peace, contentment and bliss. This book is a tool for growth, one with which you are wholly responsible for what you may gain from it.

Come now and enjoy your journey through the wisdom of the East.

The teachings of elegant sayings should be collected when one can. For the supreme gift of words of wisdom, any price will be paid.

Siddha Nagarjuna

Mindfulness

1

MINDFULNESS is the secret of life. A life lived mindfully is a life filled with peace, tranquility, joy, truth, bliss, ecstasy and compassion. Mindfulness is our direct link to the Universe. It is the solution that we have been searching for outside of ourselves since the beginning of time. The practice of mindfulness has been around for thousands of years; however, most human beings discard this approach to living and instead search for more complex and intellectual philosophies or strategies. Unfortunately, this search never seems to resolve itself. There are many individuals and texts out there that complicate and overanalyze mindfulness. This appears to be counterproductive, thus this book presents it in a practical manner in order to make it useful to anyone interested. Mindfulness is meant to be a simple, yet profound way to live. In fact, mindfulness is synonymous with authentic living.

Mindfulness is the subject of the initial section in this

book because it lays a strong foundation for everything else that follows. All the information within this book is directly related to the concept of mindfulness.

So, what exactly is mindfulness and how do you apply it to your life? Mindfulness is a form of meditation, while meditation can be more simply defined as awareness. There are many different forms of meditation but for the purpose of this book, we will specifically focus on mindfulness meditation, which involves directly participating in each moment as it occurs with complete awareness of your present experience. Life only exists in the *here and now* in this type of meditation. Mindfulness is a meditation that you can do in every second of your precious life. There is no need to escape to a secluded place, as you can practice mindfulness anywhere and at anytime, no matter what is going on around you. It's a living meditation.

Instead of presenting you with one rigid definition of mindfulness, you will find a few brief, but concise descriptions below, drawn from the wisdom of various experts and teachers of mindfulness.

Jon Kabat-Zinn, the best selling author of *Wherever You Go There You Are* and the creator of *Mindfulness Based Stress Reduction*, describes mindfulness meditation as "paying attention in a particular way; on purpose, in the present moment and non-judgmentally."

Levey and Levey in their book, *Simple Meditation and Relaxation*, state "Mindfulness liberates us from memories of the past and fantasies of the future by bringing reality of the present moment clearly into focus." They also express that "mindfulness makes us more aware of life's everyday miracles."

In one of the ancient Buddhist commentaries, it is stated that mindfulness is "presence of mind, attentiveness to the present..."

Stephen Levine, the author of *A Gradual Awakening*, says that mindfulness is a "moment to moment awareness of whatever arises, whatever exists."

Meditation teacher and author Sylvia Boorstein states that mindfulness is having "the aware, balanced acceptance of present experience. It is not more complicated than that. It is opening to or receiving the present moment, pleasant or unpleasant, just as it is, without either clinging to or rejecting it."

These descriptions use diverse expressions and terminology, but what they all share is the theory that mindfulness is being completely and fully present in life. It is being aware of what is going on within and around you in each moment of your existence. We simply practice awareness without judgment, accepting our thoughts and emotions exactly as they are.

As you may have noticed, mindfulness is a simple, yet powerful way to live. It's simply being *right here, right now.*

immersing your whole being in the present moment and fully experiencing your life. That's it! It really is that straight forward. There is no need to overanalyze, intellectualize, or complicate what it is to be mindful. Simply *be!* While there are more advanced explanations on this topic available for you to further explore through the readings listed at the end of this book, what has been described here is the simple and pure essence of mindfulness.

As you begin your journey through this book, try to bring your entire being into the present. Dive into the ocean of the Now and become intimately acquainted with the enjoyment of what is directly in front of you. As said in the Zen tradition, "When eating, eat. When walking, walk." When reading this book, it is important for you to feel open and free enough to become one with the words, to feel the presence of the teachers, and to embrace the priceless wisdom that is available to you

ARE YOU RIGHT HERE, RIGHT NOW?

If not, center yourself in the present and experience the bliss and ecstasy of the eternal moment. Enjoy your journey!

*Flow with whatever is happening and let your mind
be free. Stay centered by accepting whatever
you are doing. This is the ultimate.*

Chuang Tzu

Meditation

Mindfulness in the present moment is the key to absolute tranquility in life. Savor the brilliance and beauty of the single moment in front of you. This is where you will discover your life's meaning. Live now and become intimate with the present. Whatever it is that you attempt to do in your life today, remember to focus on the feelings it produces. Be conscious of each detail of your task and relish whatever it is you are experiencing. Excellence is sure to transpire if you put all of your energy, passion, and vitality into each specific task in each moment of your life.

Real Life Application

Begin breaking the chains of the ego and accept where you are and what you are doing right now. Dive into the harmonious and perfect rhythm of the Universe and you will experience the true essence of life. Don't resist where you are or what is going on; simply surrender to the precision of the moment and trust that you are exactly where you are supposed to be. Acceptance is the ultimate answer to all the difficulties of your life. Be RIGHT HERE, RIGHT NOW and experience all that is happening in this very moment. This is perfection!

Live as if you were to die tomorrow.

Gandhi

Meditation

Life simply consists of the present moment. Right now is truly all you possess within your life. If you desire to genuinely live, you must immerse yourself as deeply as you can within this moment. Experiencing an awakening and achieving enlightenment are only accomplished by allowing your being to be filled with the illumination and bliss of the Now. Everything other than the Now is merely an illusion that distorts your ability to truly live peacefully in the present.

Real Life Application

Do you desire to die without ever genuinely feeling as though you were finally beginning to live? So much of our time is spent feeding the ego's need to rehash the past and negatively predict the future. This is not living. This is being dragged along by the ego's leash. Let go of the attachments of the past and the desires of the future and simply BE, RIGHT NOW. This is infinite freedom and freedom is life.

*Meditate and realize this world
is filled with the presence of God.*

Upanishads

Meditation

Look around and immerse yourself in the cascade of silence and tranquility of the Universe. Basking in the stillness of the Universe will help you realize the Truth. Focus on and become one with the mysterious beauty of the sky, the innocence and love of your family, the compassion of your friends and the power and illumination of the products of creation.

Real Life Application

Many human beings shut down when they hear or read the word 'God'. This is most likely due to being pressured or 'preached to' throughout their lives. God is not synonymous with a specific religion; as Gandhi said, "God has no religion."

God is simply a term that we use to describe the invisible, intangible and mystifying force that drives the Universe. God is personal to, and within, each human being. God is within us and is that omnipotent and all-loving source that connects everything. Contemplate the characteristics of your personal God and begin to connect to this perfect energy.

The greatest revelation is stillness.

Lao Tzu

Meditation

Be still and experience the natural ecstasy of this sacred moment. Embrace the all-pervading Universal Energy that surrounds you and allow it to penetrate your entire being. This bliss you feel is the genuine nature of life. Remember that this dynamic energy is constantly available to you; you must simply allow it to enter and fuse within the heart of your genuine being.

Real Life Application

Sit in nature for an extended period of time and concentrate entirely on the connection of your breath and the air that surrounds you. This is the energy of the Universe. It is present wherever you are. Your direct link to this source is your breath; inhale, exhale; the breath of life. You are this source; if you are still and unite with the invisible energy of the cosmos, you will see, feel and become one with this miraculous force.

Learn to let go.
That is the key to happiness.

Buddha

Meditation

Throughout our lifetime, we accumulate and carry around all kinds of excess baggage. This causes suffering on a daily basis. When you let go of the past, you will begin to have the ability to savor the present moment. Release the excessive burden of the past, and experience the liberation and freedom that this gives you. You are meant, as a human being, to live each moment with tranquility and sovereignty. However, carrying the weight of your past makes this impossible.

Real Life Application

Think for a moment. Do you attach yourself to every memory and thought that floods your mind? This attachment leads to discontentment, frustration and an inability to enjoy life. You become a hostage to your mind and surrender your ability to have autonomy. Begin to free yourself from this bondage by first forgiving yourself, and then forgiving others. Try writing down your attachments to the past, then contemplate and ponder them one final time, and finally, tear them up and throw them away, burn them, or offer them to the Universe in some other creative way. The key is to rid yourself of their destructive influence, and embark upon your new found journey of freedom and tranquility.

The future depends on what we do in the present.

Gandhi

Meditation

What you do in each moment becomes the building blocks of your future. There is no reason to worry or fret about the future, just remember that you have control of each moment you live today. Create the best moments you can and your future will consist of what you desire. Discontinue your habitual need to pollute the present with regret and guilt from the past and qualms about the future. If you center yourself and exude excellence in the *Now*, the future you most desire will take care of itself.

Real Life Application

Concentrate thoroughly on the task at hand, whether it is a project at work or simply washing the dishes. Begin to develop the habit of staying completely in the moment. When the debris of the past is lurking in your mind, simply acknowledge it and let your ego know that you are not willing to allow this to ruin the gift of the present anymore. Let it pass gently without attaching yourself to the thoughts or emotions of these memories. Remember, life is made up of the present; the rest is merely an illusion. You only have now so make the very best of it.

Everything has beauty, but not everyone sees it.

Confucius

Meditation

Awaken the eyes of your soul so that you can bathe in the majestic and illuminating splendor of the Universe. Step out of the darkness of your ego and become aware of the truth contained in your spirit. Look around and notice the miraculousness in everything that surrounds you. Pay close attention and remain conscious, and soon you will become one with your surroundings, and the all encompassing beauty of the Universe.

Real Life Application

Be mindful of the beauty and perfection that surrounds you. Rid yourself of all past learning, and look at the Universe as if you were reborn and given sight for the first time. Marvel in the precise design of nature and connect with the sacred force of the Universe. This force pervades your being although it is most often overshadowed by the haze of your worldly ego. Step through this fog and enter the blissful glow of your soul.

Let us try to recognize the precious nature of each day.

His Holiness the Dalai Lama

Meditation

Let us take this quotation a bit further and realize the precious nature of each moment of our lives. This moment is all we are ever guaranteed. Life equals this moment and nothing more. Time is a dangerous illusion that deprives us of the pure bliss that fills the Now. Enlightened living takes place entirely in the Now and nowhere else. Rid yourself of the destructive past and the worrisome future, and dive into the infinite present.

Real Life Application

Concentrate and immerse yourself into what is in front of you with all your consciousness. Should anything else begin to flood your mind, quickly acknowledge it and let it go. Right here and right now is all you need to concern yourself with. Mindfulness of the task at hand can turn the ordinary experience into an extraordinary adventure. Whatever you do, do it with your entire being.

Precious and rare opportunities surround us,
and we should recognize their value.

His Holiness the Dalai Lama

Meditation
Our 'normal' daily melodramatic lives overshadow the miraculousness that surrounds us. To become one with the beauty contained in the Universe, it is imperative that you escape the dense fog of delusion and embrace the truth of the Universe. Miracles are an everyday occurrence when we live with mindfulness and according to our soul, but miracles cease to exist when we are caught in the entrapment of the ego.

Real Life Application
Be mindful and alert to the signs in your daily life. Walk slowly and look around noticing all the wonders of the Universe. Listen closely to the voice of your soul and follow this guidance, rather than quickly racing through each moment of your life to complete tedious tasks. Slow down and consciously experience everything in your path.

No matter how hard the past,
one can always begin again today.

Buddha

Meditation

Today is all we have. In fact, this moment right now is all that you ever really possess in life. If you sit and sincerely contemplate this, you will realize that you are never truly guaranteed the next moment. Your mind is determined to consistently place your attention deep within the past or far into the future. Both of these (living in the moments of the past or dreaming of the moments of the future) are illusions that destroy the reality of the present. Detach yourself from the faulty guidance of your mind and simply allow yourself to *be* in the radiance of the Now. This is where living takes place; it does not exist anywhere but in the present.

Real Life Application

When your thoughts wander, attaching themselves to the pain and regret of the past, or becoming stuck in the debilitating fear and angst of the future, simply allow those thoughts to flow gently by, without feeding them with any emotional responses or reacting impulsively. Remind yourself that they are just thoughts and that they have no basis in the reality of the present. Do not attempt to stop these thoughts; instead, just let them move along like the clouds of the heavens move swiftly above us. Come back to the present and bathe in the light of your being.

Truth

II

TRUTH IS EMBEDDED within each of our souls, lying patiently beneath the dark clouds of our egos. Seeking and practicing Ultimate Truth in our lives is a continuous process of sifting through the delusions of the ego and aligning ourselves with the principle truths of the Universe. All of creation rests on a strong foundation built upon truth that provides us with the perfect flow of energy with which to permeate the cosmos.

Truth is something that we intuitively feel and know within our beings. It is separate from intellectualization and egotistic views. When we think, believe, speak, emote, and act, we intrinsically know if we are aligned with the truth of living purely, or with the lie of the ego. Truth will always conquer delusion.

It is crucial to gain the skills necessary to discern truth from the deception of the mind and the popular opinion of what truth actually is. The majority of institutions within our society have yet to gain this understanding and, unfortunately, are governed based on the majority opinion of people's egos rather than the foundational principles of the Universe. The application of truth is certainly lacking in our world today. However, if you and I continue our search and awaken to the truth of life, we will create lasting changes and contribute to the further advancement of humanity. For each moment and each situation in your life, ask yourself if you are living according to the truth, or being dragged along by the fabrications of the ego. Earnestly look within yourself and the answer will be revealed.

There is no God greater than Truth.

Gandhi

Meditation

Truth has the power to transform humanity. Seeking and aligning oneself with the truth is the greatest task that you can perform in your lifetime. The Universe has a foundation of essential truths that it was created upon. Unfortunately, man's ego has contaminated the purity of these foundational principles and has built its own society based on a delusional philosophy of living. We must get back to the sacred principles of the Universe and trust in their divine powers.

Real Life Application

Worshiping your ego's canon will lead you to a life based on false principles. Within you lies the divine doctrine which will lead you through the doorway of enlightenment. Assess the beliefs that you live according to, and genuinely discern between what is truth, and what is delusion. Is it truth that you desire to be guided by, or are you satisfied with following the fabrications of your ego?

Believe nothing merely because you have been told it.

Buddha

Meditation

You will, of course, hear many things, some true and others false, throughout the journey of your life. It is imperative that you not take hearsay as fact, and it is of supreme importance to reflect upon all information that comes your way and seek out the truth. If you allow your inner light to assess the truth, you will certainly never go wrong. The truth is an innate part of your being. If you involve your ego, you will surely be thrown off your path.

Real Life Application

When faced with new information, it is vital to delve deeply within your own being, where the ultimate truth lies, and reflect in the solitude of nature. Within your soul are all the answers you will ever require in life. Make it a point to investigate the knowledge that is presented to you, and never rely on the so-called authority of human experts. Remember, the ego is always lurking in the background, waiting patiently to lead you away from the path of learning the truth.

The innocent who suffers insults, whips and chains,
whose weapon is endurance and whose army
is character—that person I call holy.

Buddha

Meditation

In your daily life, be sure not to simply follow popular opinion, but to also fight for the truth that lives within your soul. Truth is often unacceptable and dangerous to those living a lie. However, it is eternally noble and enlightening to challenge the lies of society and expose the truth in any way you can. This may not make you extraordinarily popular or well liked by some, but, as will be seen in the final analysis of life, you will grow and you will prosper. Most importantly, the Universe will continue to evolve.

Real Life Application

Take a risk along your journey and stand up for something you know to be the Ultimate Truth. Whether others around you like it or not, refuse to retreat. The Universe stands behind you when fighting for the core principles of living. If you believe something to be true and knowingly back down to society's delusional nature, you will lose your true self and contribute to the world's demise. Whatever you do, always seek the truth and you will be guaranteed success.

In criticizing, the teacher is hoping to teach.
That's all.

Bankei

Meditation
The ignorant and delusional minds of the world despise and immediately flinch at the smallest bit of oncoming criticism. The wise embrace and gladly welcome it. Criticism is vital nutrition for our developing soul, and it is important to remember that criticism doesn't have to be negative. All individuals that criticize you have been put in your path to aid in the further evolution of your being. When dealing with criticism, kindly thank the teacher and be grateful for the lesson.

Real Life Application
Remain mindful of each step you take on your path, as teachers constantly appear along our passage to liberation. Each being you find yourself among has something pertinent to teach you. You may choose to take this instruction as steps to a higher realm of consciousness, or you may choose to become offended and learn nothing. Whether it's the man on the highway cutting you off, the ignorant colleague that you may want to lash out at or the liberated man that shares his wisdom, each is an example of a teacher we may encounter on our pilgrimage to enlightenment. Be sure to thank them all with gratitude and exhilaration.

*It is no measure of health to be well adjusted
to a profoundly sick society.*

Chinese saying

Meditation

Adapting to society's delusions will limit your experiences in life. These false beliefs and conditioned states will leave you trapped within the cage of your mind. You will endlessly chase your desires without ever having a sense of fulfillment. Human beings continuously seek one desire after another, each one creating a seemingly endless cycle of despair. This is the diseased society that we live in. Fortunately, we always have the option of liberating ourselves from this turmoil and discovering the freedom that lies within. This freedom is found within our soul and is eternally available; we must simply make the decision to access its infinite power.

Real Life Application

It is very important to consciously appraise the path you walk each day. Do you follow society's guidance without questioning its validity, or are you tuned into the voice of your soul which always speaks the truth? To live what everyone else calls normal may be a life lived in constant illusion. Set aside society's beliefs as well as your ego's and align with the Universal Truth, then you will finally experience genuine living.

What we call reality is a dream made by the mind.

Stephen Levine

Meditation

Awaken your entire being to the truth of the Universe. Do not allow your ego to manipulate you into believing that the melodramas of the physical world are a reality in which you must participate. Always reflect deeply within your being and allow your spirit to determine what is important in your life. To follow the ego's path is to become empty. If you follow the path of the Universal Source, you will be eternally fulfilled. Discover what your spirit desires, rather than yielding to what your ego demands.

Real Life Application

Take a walk in nature and allow the truth to penetrate your being. Ponder what is real and what is a dream in your life. Is the hustle and bustle of society truly what life is about, or is there more to it than that? Seek truth everywhere you go, and do not let the delusional aspect of society convince you differently. The essence of your being eternally recognizes what is real and what is merely a dream woven by the mind.

Those who delight in truth sleep peacefully with clear minds.

Buddha

Meditation

Only when we are in direct alignment with the Way of the Universe is it possible to feel genuine peace and tranquility. Your soul only knows the truth; thus, when you permit your ego to compromise the integrity of your soul, there will be discord felt within your complete being. Human beings have this incredible, but often disastrous, ability to rationalize and fool themselves using their intellect. However, the spirit can never be deceived because it only knows the truth.

Real Life Application

Within you dwells the Ultimate Truth of the Universe. It lives within your heart and soul, but your ego constantly attempts to overshadow this force and delude your beliefs. Search deep within your being, and identify and bask within the beauty illuminating from the truth, rather than binding yourself to the chains of the ego. What lies does your ego attempt to disguise as truth in your life? The sooner you assess and realize the fallacy of these beliefs, the sooner you will become free from the gloomy and claustrophobic prison of the ego.

The Ultimate Truth is beyond words.
Doctrines are words. They're not the way.
The way is wordless. Words are illusions ...

Bodhidharma

Meditation

Our lives cannot be lived according to words or false concepts that the human intellect has invented. We must feel and embrace the truth internally and align with this powerful and trusting force. Human beings create words, while the Universe creates our ultimate reality. Deep within you lie the principles of truth that you must sense intimately with your heart rather than know with your mind. Freedom is the result of living the truth, while imprisonment is the result of living in an illusion.

Real Life Application

Take a journey into the depths of your being and it is certain that you will meet with the truth face to face. It dwells within you, patiently awaiting your arrival. You will discover it, if you are a genuine seeker. You must penetrate the veil of your ego, embracing the truth with the purity and intimacy of your entire soul. Intellect will only push you further from reality. Feel, embrace, and bond with the truth that lies within you, the truth that is waiting to be discovered and applied to your life. Quiet your intellect and be still; this is where you will discover the truth of the Universe.

You are the content of your consciousness;
in knowing yourself you will know the Universe.

Krishnamurti

Meditation

Separation from the Universe is merely an illusion fashioned by our egos. The ultimate reality remains that we are the Universe; we are one with all. Exclusivity is a product of societal thinking, and has nothing to do with the ultimate nature and course of life. Enter the enchanting realm of unity and you will discover the original and eternal nature of creation.

Real Life Application

Sit quietly and converse with the wisdom of the Universe. Allow the separation created by your ego to disappear and join in the union of all that exists. Become one with the world, the trees, the sky, and the clouds. Allow the miraculousness that surrounds you to enter your entire being and begin to feel the oneness that exists between you and your surroundings. Within this oneness there are no limits. Limitations are delusions of the ego. Go into the world and express the freedom of your true nature, demonstrating the limitless power that lives within you which is patiently waiting to be expressed.

A wise man makes his own decisions;
an ignorant man follows public opinion.

Chinese proverb

Meditation

Majority opinion in our world is based on delusion. Unconsciously following this direction and guidance will lead you away from the path of truth. Seek wisdom and truth from deep within your being and you will discover the path of illumination that your soul has prepared for you. This path transcends worldly thought and aligns itself with the Ultimate presence.

Real Life Application

Search within the depths of your pure being and discover the wisdom that lies there untouched. Feel and embrace the truth of life, and begin to apply it to your own daily journey. Rather than being caged in by the chaos and delusion of societal thinking and acting, plot your own course based on the truth you discover.

Change

III

CHANGE IS YOUR GREATEST ALLY in your personal journey toward spiritual transformation. There exists a popular saying that states, "If nothing changes, nothing changes." Thus, if you wish to change your life, society, or even the world, you must set out on a voyage of inner exploration and change. This inner voyage will ignite a process of outer change benefiting you as well as all of humanity. The most beautiful gift in life is your ability to change your course, no matter what course you have taken up until now. You must always remember that the past is no longer real, therefore, the past does not have the power to hold you back from living the life you truly aspire to live.

Along your journey toward enlightenment, significant opportunities will be presented to you. Your task is to remain awake and grasp these concepts for use on your voyage. Every moment, every trial, every obstacle, and every so-called failure, is an essential part of your soul's evolutionary process. It is imperative that you learn from everyone and everything along your path. There are no coincidences in this world; absolutely everything you experience is meant to be part of your learning experience here on Earth. Absolutely everything is the way it is supposed to be. Right here and right now, only perfection is present in your life.

When embarking on your personal change expedition, it is vital to keep a few indispensable factors in mind. The factors listed below are not all inclusive, but they will help to guide you in your quest toward personal and Universal transformation.

       Discover the unique purpose that lies within you, and pursue this quest with passion and undying determination.

       Instead of sitting back and thinking about the profound changes you desire to make in your life, get up and take action.

       Action is divided into small mindful steps that lead to your desired goal. Always remember to be present during each moment of the process, rather than obsessing over the desired goal. (Much of our life is bypassed when we engage in tunnel vision, simply seeing the end rather than being conscious of each step of the process.)

എ Change for the good of humanity, without pro-
jecting selfish outcomes.

എ Change will materialize in your life as long as you
consistently apply hard work, persistence, determination and the virtuous intention of helping
other human beings. (If your objectives are not
aimed at helping humanity, they are meaningless.)

എ Always strive for excellence, going above and
beyond what is expected of you.

Now, move forward and begin manifesting the lasting
changes you desire in your life.

You must be the change you wish to see in the world.

Gandhi

Meditation

Many people relax by sitting down to watch the nightly news or their favorite sitcom, often criticizing the world and society. The problem is that these people just keep sitting. The solution is not to sit, but to act. Take control of your life and your purpose, and begin to live it passionately. Within you is a piece of the puzzle that acts as a catalyst to transform the world. Don't just wander along the delusional path of society. Get up and act, believe, demonstrate, or do anything else that shows the world the remarkable changes that one human being can create.

Real Life Application

Contemplate the changes that you would like to see in this Universe. Be sure not to allow the pessimism and negativity of your mind to disrupt your vision for a better world. Look within and plan to make a small change within your being. Believe that this change has the potential and energy to initiate transformation within humanity. Each human being's individual actions affect the directions that the world travels. Remember, you are a powerful part of the cosmos.

The biggest room in the world is the room for improvement.

Japanese proverb

Meditation

It doesn't matter who we are (or think we are), what we do for a living, how much wealth we have amassed, what incredible achievements we have accomplished, and so forth; we continuously have room to work on growth and development. Never give up on your journey of self improvement; there are always opportunities for growth. Those who believe they have nothing to work on happen to be the individuals that require the most in-depth work.

Real Life Application

Honestly assess your inner world and define a part of you that you would like to improve. This inner quest must be sincere and complete. The first step is to shine light on those areas of darkness that you may be hiding from and acknowledge their presence. From there, you can finally accept these aspects of your being and begin working on transformation. This internal work is the core of the spiritual life.

If a thing is worth doing, it's worth doing well.

Chinese proverb

Meditation

Everything you do in your life deserves your undivided attention and 100% of your effort. This is the most effective way to seize opportunities and miracles that avail themselves to you along your daily journey. Strive to engrave your unique and precious trademark on everything you pursue in life. This encompasses everything from washing the dishes to painting a masterpiece. Each task of each moment in life is sacred and should be treated this way. Simply to be healthy enough to wake up, take a shower, vacuum, and to complete all of the other so called 'ordinary' tasks in your life, is a miracle, and each of these tasks overflows with divinity.

Real Life Application

Dedicate one entire day to focus all of your attention and energy on each and every task that you become involved in. Immerse yourself in each moment and each breath, and experience the ecstasy and power of the eternal present. Notice the energy that surrounds you, along with the serenity and tranquility of the Universe. Simply *be*, and become one with whatever you are involved in. This is life. Your presence in the *Now* is as sacred as living gets.

A fall into a ditch makes you wiser.

Chinese proverb

Meditation

Falling is a necessity on your path to success. Falling often is the direct path to enlightenment. We must stumble and fall to obtain the wisdom we have been brought here to learn. Life is filled with ditches. However, it is also covered with mountains. When stuck in a ditch, you must learn from your mistakes and continue your climb to success.

Real Life Application

Begin to adopt a different way of looking at so-called failures. Realistically, these moments in your life are growth-filled learning experiences that will eventually catapult you to the peak of success. Fall often, pick yourself up each time, and keep climbing the mountainous terrain of success. There is only one moment of true failure in life and that is when you give up.

A gem is not polished without rubbing,
nor a man perfected without trials.

Chinese proverb

Meditation

Adversity and challenges along our journey are what sculpt us into the human beings we were created to be. Without struggles and difficulties in life, our soul would decay and our life would lack meaning and purpose. Welcome each and every opportunity that comes your way, for these will further the evolution of your soul. Life is a continuous journey of growth, and the possibilities for advancement are immeasurable. Take advantage of the trials and tribulations life presents, and convert them into stepping stones toward extraordinary success.

Real Life Application

Begin to reframe the way your mind interprets or perceives difficulties and challenges in your life. If you identify something as a problem, it will unquestionably become a problem. However, if you look upon these precious times in your life as additional ingredients for your growth and evolution, then that's exactly what they'll become. Turn each obstacle in your life into what it truly is, a unique learning experience that acts as a catalyst in the transformation of your soul.

The man who removes a mountain
begins by carrying away small stones.

Chinese proverb

Meditation

Often, when we look at the entirety of any task that confronts us along our passage through life, our ego immediately fills our mind with overcomplicated messages and often defines the task as an impossibility. The ego's goal is to overwhelm you with these interpretations and, ultimately, lead you to giving up on your true purpose. The ego desires endless struggle and suffering. As a spiritual being searching for truth and awareness, you must transcend the influence of the ego and simplify your world. Simplicity is where success, peace and enlightenment are discovered. This is the essence of your being.

Real Life Application

Choose a task in your life that you often dismiss from your consciousness because of its perceived complexity. Sit down with paper and a pen, and take notes as to how this task can be broken down into smaller, more manageable steps that you can take on without much difficulty. This process can be applied to any project that you wish to embark upon. It's that simple. Stop intellectualizing and pushing yourself further away from completion, and begin taking the necessary action to progress. All great feats are done in this manner. I almost feel as if I should apologize that I don't have any great philosophical or intellectual suggestions to share with you, but try it this way, you may be pleasantly surprised.

Behind each jewel are 3000 sweating horses.

Zen saying

Meditation

Do not buy into the myth that only the 'lucky' and 'fortunate' succeed and are delivered riches. Behind all genuine success, is a sturdy foundation of hard work, determination and persistence. To become successful in a virtuous and sincere manner, one must contribute 'soul labor' to reap those immense rewards. That is to say, one must labor toward one's purpose with all of the passion and love contained within one's soul. With these vital ingredients, there is nothing that can impede you upon your path to success.

Real Life Application

Contribute your love and compassion to each task along your journey toward greatness, and you will be amazed by the gems that come your way. When you live in this manner, the Universe will act as your guide and assure you success. But remember, we are talking about genuine success, which may differ from your ego's limited definition. Thus, you must discern between the selfish success of the ego and the benevolent success of the soul. What does your ego demand? What does your soul deeply desire?

Even the deepest pool stagnates without action.

Buddha

Meditation

It is possible that you may be moving rather quickly, but not truly going anywhere. You may be standing still, even though your mind is frantic and constantly racing. In the world today, it is common practice to live with anxiety and emergencies, and really be stuck in one spot or, worse yet, be moving backward. Are you joining in with the idle chaos of society or are you moving forward in a virtuous manner?

Real Life Application

Assess the routines that are a part of your daily life and decide if these practices are genuinely moving you ahead in your spiritual evolution, pushing you back, or keeping you in the phase of stagnation. Some pertinent questions to ponder include: Are you living in the present or polluting your life while living in the past? Are you connecting with humanity or separating yourself? Are you focused on monetary and material possessions or are you seeking truth? Is your life based on purpose and meaning or are you wandering about following the guidance of the deluded society you live in? Do your best to discern the answers given by your pure being, as well as your selfish ego.

Non-violence requires much more courage than violence.

Gandhi

Meditation

Violence seems to be a common way of life these days. We are entertained daily by violence on television, the movie screens, and in all facets of the media. We hear about it, read about it, are involved in it, and we sit back and let it persist. It appears that violence is the new standard or philosophy of living according to the popular or majority opinion. Is this the way you desire the Universe to evolve? If your answer is no, stand up and do something about this downward spiral. Violence is merely another delusion that our society has taken a hold of. In the end, violence simply creates more violence. It is never an appropriate solution; violence is just part of the problem.

Real Life Application

Rather than closing your eyes and ears to the violence that is taking place around you, become part of the solution. Ignoring what is going on in the world around you causes just as much of a problem as those acting out in violence. Determine how you can take non-violent action to help contribute to the reversal of society's current path. It may be as simple as writing a letter, teaching a young person effective non-violent coping skills, or mentoring an at-risk youth. You decide, but please don't just sit back—take action.

Opportunities are multiplied as they are seized.

Sun Tzu

Meditation

Each moment of each day has embedded in it limitless opportunities for growth and development. Immerse yourself in the vast ocean of the Now and avail yourself to the infinite possibilities out there waiting for you. Each time you are successful in a task you take on, you will be presented with a subsequent gift from the Universe. You must keep your eyes open and follow the signs that are placed upon your path.

Real Life Application

'Coincidences' are plentiful in our lives, but are these occurrences merely coincidences? Unfortunately, your ego desires that you believe in the coincidence theory and quickly discard the events as chance happenings. Following your ego is the easiest way to be blind to the signs of the Universe. Behind these so called 'coincidental events' is the powerful and profound intelligence of creation. These are divine events created with the purpose of aligning you with the Ultimate Truth. You must keep the eyes of your soul open in order to bathe in cosmic synchronicity. Connect to this source, and you will eternally walk the sacred path that is directly in front of your eyes.

Ego / Illusion

IV

OUR EGO IS A HIGHLY sophisticated mechanism which attempts to successfully cast its veil of deceit over the luminous and enlightened nature of our soul. The ego's ultimate goal is to persuade us that it is a genuine reflection of who we are. It presents itself through false thoughts, feelings and deluded beliefs about the true nature of reality. The ego is cunning and devious, so we must be aware of its potential influence at all times. Most individuals travel along their entire journey of life believing they are what their ego tells them they are. This is, in fact, the most destructive delusion of all. We are certainly not our ego, nor our thoughts, nor are we our beliefs. We are perfect spiritual beings that often allow the ego to tell us differently.

Let us take a brief look at the distinct qualities of the ego as compared to the soul, or pure essence, of our beings.

& The ego creates separation; the soul is united with the entire Universe.

ം The ego creates limitations; the soul knows no boundaries.

ം The ego is governed by illusion; the soul knows nothing but truth.

ം The ego has infinite external desires and demands; the soul has everything it needs.

ം The ego dwells in the past and future; the soul eternally inhabits the present.

ം The ego clouds our true essence; the soul is our true essence.

You always have the freedom of choice when deciding which path you wish to follow; the path governed by the ego or the path illuminated by the soul. You can certainly continue your endless and manic search for happiness outside of yourself, or you can follow the wise and gentle guidance of your soul. Rest assured, it is indeed possible to escape the suffering and chaos created by the ego. We can definitely resist the powerful force that drags us into the illusory world. I urge you to begin your sacred journey of freedom immediately, without hesitation, and to align your personal path with the Universal principles of the soul. Quiet your ego, and enter the blissful realm of your deepest self.

*It can be said that God cannot be known in the mind
but only experienced in the heart.*

Stephen Levine

Meditation

Faith in what exists beyond the physical sphere resides in
our heart and soul, and can only be sensed by the pure
nature of our being. Our intellect is controlled by our ego.
This is something we need to transcend to begin deeply
experiencing the Universe without intellectualizing the
experience away. Not having a full understanding of the
divine source is just how it is meant to be—this allows you
to develop hope and faith in the mysteries of the Universe,
as well as the opportunity to transform your physical
being into a spiritually enlightened entity. Not knowing
and accepting the fact that you don't have to know, are
vital keys to spirituality.

Real Life Application

Stop your racing mind for a few moments, and genuinely
connect with the power of the Universe. Feel the energy,
the omnipotence and the wisdom that exists in our natural
environment. Align your heart and soul with this potent
force, and put all of your trust into the very soul of the
Universe; and remember, to not know is the way it is
intended to be.

Pleasure does not make us happy.

Stephen Levine

Meditation

The fleeting sensory pleasures created by material and corporeal possessions will not fulfill your inner yearning for happiness and tranquility. The blissful state you seek is already within you as a natural part of your being and must be tapped into consciously. Absolutely nothing outside of your being will provide you with genuine contentment. You may continue in this useless search externally, but know that it has no end.

Real Life Application

Think back to when you acquired something you really desired and longed for. Does it still provide you with genuine happiness on a daily basis, or has it been replaced by additional desires? Do you truly believe that transitory pleasures will ever give you lasting happiness? Begin to embark on your inner expedition to uncover the happiness that is the inherent essence of your being. This happiness is present in each and every moment we are alive and breathing; it is up to you to recognize and tap into its potential.

Cease this very moment to identify yourself with the ego.

Shankara

Meditation

Thoughts that manifest within your ego are not related to who you truly are. We are not our thoughts, we are not our ego, and we are not who society tells us we are. We are simply a reflection of the soul of the Universe, which consists of the entirety of humanity. We are connected to everyone and everything that surrounds us. Once we realize this, we can begin to break through the illusion created by society and our ego, and only then can we enter the harmonious flow of energy that surrounds us.

Real Life Application

Up until this very moment, you may have lived your life believing that you are what your ego identifies you as. This is a falsehood that must be corrected. You are a pure being that is one with all. To align with the Universal energy within you, you must slowly begin to detach from the fabricated-self that the ego has created. When you begin to pull aside the veil of your ego, it is then that you discover the perfection that is present in the core of your being. Take it slow, but begin to chip away at the membrane of delusion that your ego has preserved for far too long. Right here, right now, you are receiving the message to transcend the call of the ego and to fill yourself with spiritual energy.

The self and the contents of the mind are completely separate. Our usual experience, which is directed to outer fulfillment, fails to distinguish between them.

Yoga Sutras of Patanjali

Meditation
Your search for pleasure in external objects, events and individuals is a perpetual cycle with no satisfying outcome. It eternally leaves you hollow and unfulfilled, remaining lost in the void of your corporeal being. This is the great delusion that countless human beings are mistakenly guided by on a daily basis. Escape the murkiness of the mind and discover the truth that lies within the clarity of your essential being.

Real Life Application
Separation between the 'real you' and the 'delusional you' is imperative along your spiritual journey. To truly believe the fabrications of the mind concerning your being is to lose much of what genuinely constitutes life. Begin your journey within, and identify the essential being that awaits your companionship. Listen closely to the whisper of your soul, rather than being carelessly pulled along by your illusive mind. Slowly shift your focus from peripheral sensory pleasures to the internal bliss that is everlasting.

When the mind comes out of the self, the world appears.

Ramana Maharshi

Meditation

To rid our being of the delusional mind is a task only a few pursue, and sadly, even fewer achieve. This is unfortunate; when our mind is still, we begin to awaken to the precious nature of all that surrounds us. Open the eyes of your soul, and bathe in the luminosity and purity of the Universe.

Real Life Application

Relax your body, mind and soul while you are in your favorite setting. This may be a room in your home, next to a stream in the woods, on the beach, or walking on a serene wooded path in nature. This place is your special place of retreat. If you don't have a serene environment to go to in order to experience peace and tranquility, search for one immediately. Embark upon a journey of stilling your mind and allowing the Universe to permeate your being within this special place. Slowly begin to transition this state to all environments in your life. In the end, you will have the capacity to experience tranquility even in the most chaotic of situations; this is your great power.

Freedom from desire leads to inward peace.

Lao Tzu

Meditation

Infinite desires permeate our daily lives causing endless misery. We achieve one thing and then move on to the next. We make our dream purchase, then we miraculously discover we must have something bigger and better. When we meet our true soul mate, we may just as suddenly find another. This senseless search for perfection and bliss outside of ourselves will never end. All that these desires do is pull you away from the precious moment that is life itself.

Real Life Application

Liberation from all desires may never be a reality in your lifetime. However, putting constant effort toward a more internally fulfilling life, through minimizing your desires, is definitely a realistic endeavor and will ultimately lead to total enlightenment. Begin pondering the nature of your desires and attachments, and be sure to honestly contemplate their effects on your inner life. Are your possessions, desires and cravings adding to your spiritual journey or taking away from it? Are you winning the race toward success or are you losing yourself in the process?

In antiquity men studied for their own sake;
nowadays men study for the sake
of impressing others.

Confucius

Meditation

Genuine fulfillment or satisfaction in life is never discovered when you exist for the benefit of others. Living for others is the simplest way to become depressed, frustrated and hollow. What other human beings think, believe, or even say about you, is not reality. However, the issue remains that we tend to make it our reality. Search within your being and truly come to know the genuine nature of *you*, then the thoughts, beliefs, words or actions of others will not even enter your consciousness.

Real Life Application

Embark on a journey of developing an intimate relationship with the real you and align yourself with the pure nature of your being. Do not allow the egos of others to affect you negatively, or push you to conform to false views of life and the Universe. There exists no spiritual growth in living your life for others, but if you live your life according to the essence of your natural being, you will undeniably inspire others to begin living their life in this same profoundly virtuous manner.

Tame the one enemy within, which is delusion.

The First Dalai Lama

Meditation

Delusion is the powerful force that is responsible for all suffering in our lives. We walk endlessly and unconsciously each day; feeding into and empowering this delusion that keeps us chained to transitory sensual pleasures, rather than tapping into the pure bliss and ecstasy that resides within our soul. It is the deluded being who chases desires endlessly and never experiences the truth or beauty of life.

Real Life Application

You must look closely at your life and sincerely recognize the delusions that guide your current existence. At first, they may appear to be steadily grounded in reality due to your ego's commitment to these false beliefs, but if you honestly and openly examine these distortions of the ego, the wisdom within you will never lie. It is your main task from this point on to free yourself from the manacles of this enemy by simply living according to the wisdom of your soul.

The ego's essence is limitation.

Swami Ajaya

Meditation

Do not dwell within the ego's boundaries. Step outside this deceptive and self-serving cage and enter the infinite light of the truth. You must always realize that you are not your ego, you are one with the infinite perfection of the Universe. In this Universe there are no walls or boundaries, there are simply endless possibilities. Venture out freely and often, exploring the freedom and tranquility that exists beyond the prison of the ego.

Real Life Application

Try this experiment: monitor the conversations of your ego for just three hours of your day. Be sure to keep some paper close by so you can jot down what it is your ego is telling you. What judgments does it make? Is it supportive of your efforts in life? What does it say about who you are? Is it positive or negative? Does it motivate you or criticize you? This is only a small sampling of questions you can answer. It is vital to listen closely and attend to what is going on inside of you. After this experiment, decide if you desire to live according to your ego, or if you wish to tap into the wisdom and radiance of your soul.

Taming the mind is the most important task of one's life.

His Holiness the Dalai Lama

Meditation
Calming the turbulence of the mind and ceasing its infinite desires will allow you to properly perceive the ultimate reality of the Universe. The mind will lead you down endless paths, with the exception of the path of truth. Embark upon a journey of detaching from your mind and aligning yourself with the inner stillness and acumen of your soul.

Real Life Application
Begin to monitor the working process of your mind. Be conscious of each thought, but do not attach yourself to these thoughts. Allow a thought to come and then flow quietly away, like a leaf floating by on the glistening stream of your consciousness. Your thoughts are not who you are, they are simply thoughts. When we attach our identity to the mind and ego, we get lost in the chaos they contain. Begin to observe your thoughts without permitting them to manage your life. Sit in the stillness of the Universe and listen closely to its guidance; it's the soft compassionate whisper within your heart that will lead you to liberation and enlightenment.

Our True Nature

V

A SACRED TREASURE awaits your discovery if you cease your external search for happiness and commence upon your internal journey. Everything that you truly desire in your life is already available at the core of your being. Within you exists infinite happiness, eternal peace, everlasting tranquility and ecstatic bliss. You entered this world as a perfect spiritual specimen. Your true nature or essence, your heart, is nothing less than supreme perfection. Everything you are looking for can be found within.

It is possible that you do not believe in any of this; there is a very logical reason for this skeptical apprehension. From the moment of your birth, your ego has been on a mission to overshadow your inherent perfection; your ego desires for you to forget the truth of your essential nature and follow its destructive and delusional path filled with desire and attachment. Your ego simply wishes you to remain a victim of the endless cycle of suffering we know as normal living. Of course, this philosophy of existence only appears 'normal' because the majority of the world operates under the bureaucracy of the ego.

Fortunately, you have a choice; you can live according to this deluded sense of self, or discover the perfection that encompasses your being. From this moment forward, you can wake each morning with the clear intention of living your sacred life in alignment with the fundamental nature of your being. You can make the firm decision to restrict your journey to one of inner exploration rather than remain on your never ending external quest. This inner path is where you will unearth the priceless treasures of freedom, liberation and pure joy.

Look within, the secret is inside you.

Hui-Neng

Meditation

Everything you will ever need along your passage through life exists within the inner recesses of your being. You are supplied with all the resources, maps, blueprints, and energy you need to live a peaceful and purposeful life. You must work diligently and navigate according to your higher self to fulfill your role here on Earth. Definitive answers to your 'why' questions (those of existence, happiness, peace, or purpose in your life) will forever be beyond your reach because they simply do not exist outside of yourself. All of this information resides within you; you may just have to clean up your internal clutter to discover the keys that will unlock your limitless potential.

Real Life Application

Relax and dive into the inner ocean of your being; realize the full potential that resides there. Contemplate your connection to the soul of the Universe and imagine the possibilities that would be available to you if only you were to put this force to work in your life. When searching within, be sure to look within your core being rather than asking your ego. Your ego exists according to limits and selfishness, while your soul lives according to the vast energy of the cosmos. When you search for the purity and essence of your being, what is it that you find?

One who returns to his nature and adheres to it, is worthy.

Chou Tun-i

Meditation

Your authentic being longs to return home to its purest nature. It desires to connect to the totality of the Universe and embrace all of humanity. Your soul desires nothing less than unconditional love and compassion. All of this resides within your being, but is hidden by the distortions created by the ego. Rid yourself of the false beliefs of the ego, and return home to the clarity and innocence of your spiritual perfection.

Real Life Application

Return home to the bliss of your genuine being. The essence of you and the whole of humanity is perfection, which is simply veiled by the clouds of the ego. Your personal guide back to the native land of your being is your soul. Listen to its soft whispers and be aware of the subtle signs presented to you. You will then return to the ecstasy and perfection of your essence.

When people reach their highest perfection
it is nothing special;
it is their normal condition.

Hindu saying

Meditation

We always seem to be striving to reach self-actualization, enlightenment and perfection. What we fail to actually realize is the fact that perfection exists within us naturally. We are born into this world perfect, free and liberated. It is our developing ego that tears us away from this blissful state, dragging us into the tyranny of its delusions. Our task is to re-discover our perfection and allow the light of our beings to once again radiate throughout the Universe like the rays of the brilliant sun.

Real Life Application

Uncover and expose the shadows your ego casts that conceal the vivacity and luminosity of your essential being. Make notes of the deceptive patterns that your ego tries to use to its advantage and begin to sever your attachments to these illusions that prevent you from reaching freedom. Ask yourself what it is that overshadows the fundamental nature of your being.

Our original nature is pure
as long as it is free from false thought.

Hui-Neng

Meditation

When we are born into this world, we consist only of purity and innocence. Our soul chooses a path to travel throughout our lifetime. However, society attempts to obstruct this path, and impede upon our destined journey. The path you are meant to travel along eternally exists within your authentic being. Your ultimate task is to clear away the debris and delusion that has been instilled by society, and join hands with your sacred purpose.

Real Life Application

False thoughts and beliefs pervade our lives, and are encouraged by the society that surrounds us. The only way we can release ourselves from the false, and enter into the truth, is by monitoring our thoughts and beliefs through contemplation, and seeking to align with the genuine principles of the Universe. Look within your being, assess which false thoughts are leading you away from your true self, and make a conscious decision to correct these distorted views.

*Happiness is your nature. It is not wrong to desire it.
What is wrong is seeking it outside when it is inside.*

Ramana Maharshi

Meditation
Deep within the core of your heart lives a precious jewel that
sparkles with pure illumination, radiating unconditional
love and compassion throughout the entire Universe. This
internal treasure is often overlooked in our lives due to
the ego's negative influence. The dark clouds of the ego
often block the glow of this brilliant jewel. What is this
jewel? The answer is simple; this jewel is *You*. Uncover
this precious gemstone and allow it to glisten in its sheer
beauty to all of those with whom you come into contact.

Real Life Application
Where do you search for happiness in your life? I would
be willing to bet that the majority of the time you search
is spent outside of yourself, focused on the external objects
and people of the world. The surprising irony of life is that
you already possess happiness, as well as all of the other
feelings for which you endlessly search. They are already
within you. Discontinue your superficial mission for peace
and happiness, and initiate your inner journey; this journey
is the ultimate destination for eternal contentment.

*Our essential nature is usually overshadowed
by the activity of the mind.*

Yoga Sutras of Patanjali

Meditation

Our mind is the creative spinner of the difficulties in our life. If we simply live aligned with the purity of our soul, our life flows along according to the Universe's principles. Your life will not endlessly become contaminated with judgment, desires, anger, hate, selfishness, or any of the other impure energies of the ego. Escape the bondage of the ego and gently allow yourself to dance in line with the rhythm of the Universe.

Real Life Application

Try detaching from your mind for an hour, and closely observe your experience. When a thought comes to you, merely let it flow by and follow the guidance of your essential being. What are your feelings? What thoughts keep popping up? How does it feel to not have to be in control of everything? For this one hour, simply *be*. Let go of all that you think you have to be or do. Let spontaneity and mindfulness guide your being.

Be master of mind rather than mastered by mind.

Zen saying

Meditation

It is imperative along our journey in life that we learn to use our mind as a beneficial instrument, rather than being victimized by its deceit and fury. Our mind is not who we are. However, it will attempt to convince you that it is your true nature. Do not be fooled. Your pure nature lies within your soul. It is up to you to embrace and align yourself with your authentic and liberated being.

Real Life Application

Establish a practice in your life where you can sit quietly observing the contents and process of your mind. Gain insight and knowledge concerning the workings of your mind, and begin to use it as a tool rather than being pulled along by its erroneous views and perceptions. Do not attach to your thoughts, or judge them when conducting this exercise. Simply notice them and allow them to gently drift away.

People become what they expect themselves to become.

Gandhi

Meditation
Believing in yourself, with all of your heart, is the principle factor to genuine success and enlightenment in life. Discard the beliefs and expectations of those around you, and embrace the infinite possibilities that have always existed within the natural state of your being. Whatever you desire from life is within your reach. It is simply a matter of realizing that you deserve it.

Real Life Application
It may seem strange, but many people do not have an answer to the following fundamental question: What do you want out of life? Can you answer this? If you can clearly visualize, and see exactly what it is that you desire, then you are on the right path. On the other hand, if you feel lost in the chaos of life, lacking direction and purpose, then the time has come to sit down and contemplate your true purpose in life. This involves searching within and listening to the voice of the Universe. Within your inner core exists the path that you are destined to follow. Be still and it will reveal itself.

When you are content to be simply yourself
and don't compare or compete,
everybody will respect you.

Lao Tzu

Meditation

One of the greatest lessons in life is to recognize that your true nature is perfect without you doing anything to make it so. The only things that steer you away from this reality are the delusions that you have adopted from society. Perfection and liberation are at the bottom of the illusory pile of debris that your ego has created. Uncover these gems, allowing them to emit their light and love throughout all of humanity.

Real Life Application

Remove the mask that you wear to adapt and conform to society's way. This is not reality and it merely drags you further away from the ultimate meaning of life. The illusive way that we are taught and conditioned throughout our lifetime clouds our ability to truly align ourselves with 'the one true way'. Uncover the precious being that you have been hiding, and live right now as you, without competition, without comparison, and without conforming to the fallacies embraced by society. Live, love, sing, dance, and enjoy the free spirit that has been stuffed in the box of the ego's delusions for way too long.

Within your own house dwells the treasure of joy;
so why do you go begging from door to door?

Sufi saying

Meditation

Searching outside of ourselves for happiness is a never-ending and unsatisfying detour along our ultimate path to enlightenment. If you choose this course, it is certainly a long and arduous path to travel. Fortunately, you have the option to embark on an inward journey that will put you back on the path of genuine contentment and inner peace. Within you exists the most exquisite treasure patiently waiting to be discovered. Go now and unearth the jewels of your pure being.

Real Life Application

Think about the path you have been traveling on thus far in your life. Do you appreciate and honor the gifts that are present within you, or are you continuously seeking external pleasure? Do you value your family and friends, and the connection you have to humanity, or do you take these things for granted? Sincerely and honestly assess your way of living, and begin making the necessary changes *right now*! Keep in mind that you will never discover the peace and happiness you desire in an external object, situation or human being. It must be, and can only be, found within.

Unity / Oneness

VI

THROUGHOUT THIS ENTIRE Universe exists an all encompassing, all loving, and omniscient flow of energy that unites everyone and everything. The Taoists describe it in the following way:

> *The great Tao flows everywhere ... All things depend on it for life, and it does not turn away from them. One may think of it as the mother of all beneath heaven. We do not know its name, but we call it TAO ... Deep and still it seems to have existed forever.*

This potent and unconditionally loving energy flows infinitely, connecting all of life, and is readily accessible to you if you make the choice to align yourself with it. Unfortunately, we are conditioned to ignore the interdependence and connectedness that is pervasive in this Universe. Our mind seeks to detach itself from this oneness, and to live in its own separate 'box' with a belief system consisting of superiority, inferiority, ignorance, a judgmental attitude and the senseless ambition to create exclusivity at all costs. These delusional beliefs that we grasp onto so tightly will ultimately annihilate humanity. Humanity cannot evolve if we proceed to exclude human beings based on external characteristics and qualities. We must join in with the Universal consciousness, and unite ourselves as the one race we belong to. We have the responsibility to begin living our ultimate purpose—to realize our underlying connection and begin helping one another in any way possible.

My challenge to you is to contemplate this divine union, and sincerely apply it in your daily life. Establish your link with this vast field of energy, and allow it to transform your life into a purposeful journey, overflowing with unconditional love, compassion, kindness and human intimacy. Transcend the confines of the ordinary, submerging yourself into this expansive dimension of possibilities and miraculous happenings. Practice unity in your every step and eliminate exclusivity from your thoughts and actions.

Nature does not hurry, yet everything is accomplished.

Lao Tzu

Meditation

Be patient in the Now, and allow the Universe to guide you. Rid yourself of the urgency and anxiety that inundates your life, and allow yourself to sense the calming effects of being centered with nature. Life was not created to be full of stress, anxiety, hatred, fear, worry, or any of the other detrimental energies that bombard us on a daily basis. Humans created this way of life, and society continues to live this way; we blindly follow along. Come back to the natural course of the Universe, rejoicing in the peace and tranquility of life. It is not necessary to take part in society's chaotic philosophy of living.

Real Life Application

What would it be like to adopt the pace of nature, and join into the harmony of the Universe? By aligning ourselves with the flow of energy that surrounds us, we surrender to the precision and harmony of nature, becoming in tune with the rhythm of the divine. Sit quietly in a special place and feel the vibrations of nature run through your being like a river flowing through the peaceful countryside. When you are one with the perfect dance of life, you will experience the peace contained within the trees, the sky, the grass, and all of nature's sacred creations. Become one with the Universe's living masterpiece.

Stop clinging to your personality and see all beings as yourself. Such a person could be entrusted with the whole world.

Lao Tzu

Meditation

To truly comprehend and honor the union of all human beings is the most astonishing and brilliant insight that one can ever have. The human race and the entire world are united as one, and this will eventually be revealed to all of humanity. However, the sooner you realize this for yourself, and begin applying it to your life, the sooner you will manifest change both in yourself and the world around you. Begin living this vital and transformative revelation today.

Real Life Application

Take a walk in nature and enter into communion with all that you experience. Become a part of the landscape; enter the comforting flow of the wind, and picture yourself as one with the far off horizon. All that exists is one. The Universe depends on the cooperation and interdependence of everything and everyone working together. Allow yourself to participate in the harmonious beating heart of the Universe.

No culture can live if it attempts to be exclusive.

Gandhi

Meditation

Currently, the state of the Universe is disheartening and full of suffering due to the presence of a single destructive force. This force is exclusivity; in other words, our idea of being separated is based on outside characteristics and excludes valuable human beings because of physical and ego-driven traits. This state of mind is pathetic and insane. The only principle that can save us from the devastating effects of this exclusivity is the purity of love. This means a demonstration of love for the totality of humanity, as well as embracing the unity and oneness of all living beings.

Real Life Application

Contemplate this phenomenon of exclusivity and honestly assess its validity. Does this idea make any sense at all? Does being a different color, different religion, or different ethnicity make a human being any better or worse than the next one? Begin to live your life embracing the connectedness of humanity. Transcend the notion of physical differences, and break down the barriers that you build to separate yourself from your fellow humans. This will surely bring a lasting change in your life, and greatly affect the state of the Universe.

The Universe has never separated itself from man.
Man separates himself from the Universe.

Lu Hsiang Shan

Meditation

Maintain your powerful connection with the source of creation, and you will soon realize the absolute unity of all life. There is a spectacular and omnipotent energy that vibrantly flows through everyone and everything around you. It is never necessary to travel alone in life; the caring and compassionate force of the Universe exists and is available to you ad infinitum. Your responsibility to yourself is to remain in constant communication with this inspiring power during each and every moment of your life.

Real Life Application

There is one and only one heartbeat that connects the totality of the cosmos. This Universal heartbeat exists ubiquitously, and is accessible to you each moment of your existence. The choice belongs to you whether you decide to commune with the heart of the Universe, or exist alone in the empty and lifeless vacuum of your ego. What will you decide?

You are the content of your consciousness;
in knowing yourself you will know
the Universe.

Krishnamurti

Meditation
Separation from the Universe is merely an illusion, fashioned by your ego. The ultimate reality remains that we are the Universe, and we are one with all. Exclusivity is a product of societal thinking and has nothing to do with the ultimate nature of life. Enter the magical realm of unity and you will discover the unique and eternal nature of creation.

Real Life Application
Within you lies all of the contents of the Universe. Creation and evolution is at the very core of your being. You contain an imprint of the Universal memory, and have instant access to this profound knowledge. When you dive into the vastness of your being and experience the brilliance it contains, you will then experience the calming waters of the majestic and eternal sea of the Universe. These infinite waters are there to provide warmth and comfort for your soul. Immerse yourself and become one with all that exists.

When you encounter someone greater than yourself,
turn your thoughts to become his equal.
When you encounter someone lesser than you,
look within and examine your own self...

Confucius

Meditation

When we awaken, there exists no superior or inferior human being. We recognize that we are all the same. The delusions that we often base our life upon are created by our exclusive ego that seeks to detach itself from the unified energy of the cosmos. Oneness is the ultimate reality of this Universe. There is no competition, no separation, and no difference between you and the remainder of humanity.

Real Life Application

Be sure to not position yourself above, or below, any other human being that walks this Earth. If we separate ourselves from the natural equality of creation, we set ourselves up for endless pain and suffering, ultimately obstructing our own purposeful journey. Tune into the similarities that exist among all human beings and join hands in the harmonious rhythm of living. To recognize the oneness of humanity is to release unconditional compassion for all. Discover your true self and you will discover the ultimate reality of the Universe.

Many do not know that we are here in this world
to live in harmony.

Buddha

Meditation

All beings that inhabit this world belong to the one soul of the Universe. We are part of one all encompassing Universal dance that contains nothing but a desire for harmony and peace. Genuine existence knows nothing but tranquility and togetherness although the darkness of our ego blocks this from occurring. Now is the time that you must take responsibility for your part of the dance and help bring the Universe back to its natural harmonious state of being.

Real Life Application

If you desire harmony in your life, it's as simple as choosing it in every single moment. It is abundantly available to you. There is no need to search outside of yourself, as it is the very foundation of this Universe. What is needed is a decision on your part to dismiss your ego's obsessions with competition, desire, attachment and judgments. You must allow these clouds of illusion to disappear from your life and, instead, you must invite harmony into each thought, feeling and action.

All things are one.

Tchuang-Tzu

Meditation

There is one fundamental principle that guides the entirety of the Universe. This principle is unity. We are intimately connected to the totality of all creation, yet we build fences, construct barriers, create labels, and utilize infinite strategies to separate ourselves from one another as much as possible. Why? Well, the simple explanation is that our ego seeks to be special. The fact remains that we are a very special and unique piece of the Universe's puzzle, without being superior to anyone, or anything.

Real Life Application

If you want peace, if you want happiness, and if you want freedom, it is vital to live according to this critical principle of unity. This is definitely a shift of paradigms if you compare it to the way the majority of humanity exists. You can easily begin to practice this sacred principle by removing your mask of superiority, breaking down the walls of your ego and practicing compassion for your fellow human beings on a regular basis. Practice the principle of oneness, and you will come to know peace and, most important of all, you will manifest peace in everything you do.

*Like the body that is made up of different limbs and organs,
all mortal creatures exist depending upon one another.*

Hindu proverb

Meditation

We, as human beings, are all traveling in the same vessel,
and are all on the same journey we know as 'life'. Wouldn't
it be nice if we could join hands in this journey, helping
one another through the struggles and challenges of life,
and enjoy our success together, as a whole? Reach out your
hand, and experience the peace and ecstasy in uniting with
the human race, as we collectively live together and help
one another. The essence of spirituality is our connection
with the world around us.

Real Life Application

Many of us live our lives competing against one another,
comparing achievements, battling, judging, and living in
opposition with our fellows rather than living with, and aiding
in human evolution. This is a lonely and frustrating existence.
Creating your own little world, and closing yourself off to
everyone but the very few you trust and approve of, is not
what the journey of life was meant to be. We are social beings,
who are intended to live in harmony with an interconnected
purpose; a purpose consisting of the ultimate evolution of
humankind. Embark upon a journey of expanding your
little closed-off world, and invite others in. Meet new people,
explore your prejudices, and connect with the divinity presented by the sheer diversity of human beings.

No snowflake ever falls in the wrong place.

Zen saying

Meditation

There exists one all encompassing word that describes the totality of creation; this word is *perfection*. Everyone and everything is united as one perfect Universal entity. This rhythmic connection never goes wrong. When we connect to this source and discard the false beliefs of the ego, we align ourselves with our precise path, and we too cannot go wrong. Our will and ego are impediments upon our journey. It is up to us to tame these beasts and follow the course of the perfect Universal energy.

Real Life Application

There are many paths we can follow during our lives, as mapped out by our beliefs, desires and views of how the world operates. Look intently at the path you are currently traveling, and decide if this is the path of your soul, or the path of your ego. One easy way to discern which path you are on is to take a look at your relationship with the world around you. Are you an exclusive person who separates yourself from others or do you embrace your connection with all of humanity? Do you believe there is a single purpose in the Universe or is it just that the 'strongest' survive? Are you connected to all of life or are you a separate being, busy selfishly clawing your own way to the top?

Simplicity

VII

L AO TZU OFFERS US the following recipe for
living a satisfying and successful life: "Manifest plain-
ness, embrace simplicity, reduce selfishness, and have few
desires." Regrettably, our lives, our societies, and our world
are much more complex than this, and, generally operate
in a completely opposite manner.

You may say, 'That's just the way it is' or, 'That's the way
this world functions'. I would then respond by explaining
that it doesn't have to be this way; we can choose to embrace
the beauty and richness of simplicity, and live more serene
and satisfying lives. Has the complex and gluttonous
nature of society added to the contentment and peace of
mind of the individuals living in it? If we are honest with
ourselves, the answer is definitely and undeniably 'no',
and, in fact, it appears that the more complex, high tech,
and externally-based society becomes, the more frequently
problems seem to arise. What's the answer then? Well, I
believe *simplicity* offers a solution to our dilemma.

Simplicity is the essence of any spiritual practice. To over complicate, over accumulate and over analyze, leaves us with an underlying feeling of being overwhelmed. This anxious and frantic state of mind is made up of ruinous delusions that will subtly lead you away from all that is spiritual. To simply be, living devoid of all the chaos caused by external demands, is the path to ultimate liberation and pure joy.

This simplicity dwells within the core of your being. It's the simplicity that we once experienced as innocent and inquisitive children, first appreciating the simple beauty and wonder of all of our surroundings. It is living in the moment, feeling all of the bliss and ecstasy that the Universe has to offer us. Exploring the world with complete faith, without debilitating worry, regret, anxiety, self consciousness, and all other remaining conditioned states we have adopted from society. Simplicity is enjoying the pure essence of a beautiful object and feeling the 'specialness' within it, without having to amass a pile of all the best objects in the world in order to feel worthy. To become a simple and innocent child again, is to become a spiritual being.

Simplicity is not easy to apply in our overly intricate and intellectual world, but it is indeed feasible. We must gently slip away from all the ego's desires and demands, and begin to recognize that life is not how large our salary is, how much knowledge we amass, how big and exquisite our home is, or how many and, what type of, cars we drive. Similar to what was discussed in the mindfulness section at the beginning of this book, life is simply our being present; it is being in the here and now, completely accepting who we are, what we have, and believing that this is all we require for genuine peace and happiness in our lives. Simplicity is a powerful tool that rewards you greatly right from the start.

Thich Nhat Hanh offers a suggestion that will help you to apply simplicity in your own life:

> *Do not accumulate wealth while millions are hungry ... Live simply and share time, energy, and material resources with those in need.*

If you realize that you have enough, you are truly rich.

Tao Te Ching

Meditation

Our insatiable appetite for more and more has no conclusion. It is a continuous cycle of suffering, which only leads to an intensified hunger, more anxiety, and greater frustration. It simply leaves us with a bigger and bigger void each time we travel around this destructive cycle. This craving is created within the ego, and is detached from the spirit. It is imperative to abandon the ceaseless yearning of the ego, and align yourself with the perfect energy of your true nature. This is where you will discover satisfaction and genuine serenity.

Real Life Application

What is 'enough' in your life? Unfortunately, only you can determine that. Only you can set the bar. You may labor under the illusion that the more and more you achieve and possess, the happier and more satisfied you will become. That path is always an option. However, if you are open and honest with yourself, you have the insight to understand the suffering that this philosophy has created in your life. Your alternative is to allow the illumination of the truth to peak through the clouds of your ego, coming to an acceptance and understanding that more is not better. Discover the peace, tranquility, and satisfaction that the practice of simplicity brings to your life.

A tree that fills the span of a man's arms grows
from a downy tip; a terrace nine stories high
rises from handfuls of earth; a journey
of a thousand miles, from beneath one's feet.

Lao-Tzu

Meditation

Great feats begin with an initial leap and are created one small step at a time. Anything worth manifesting in life begins with a thought, followed by a specific action, a little at a time. Great masterpieces are small works that have been combined into greatness. Celebrated works are never fantasized and then miraculously produced; they are all a work of determination, persistence and patience. Believe and visualize in your own personal work of genius, and become one with the celestial source if you wish to manifest it in the physical world.

Real Life Application

Magnificent works of brilliance are all created from simplicity. Overwhelming ourselves with the intricacy and complexity of unnecessary tasks in our life is the easiest way to fall into the trap of procrastination and stagnation. Any task, whether ordinary or extraordinary, consists of simple steps from the beginning to the end. Create a life of simplicity and live completely in the eternal present, then you can truly possess all that you have ever imagined. Most importantly, you will have discovered the peace and contentment that lies in living the simple life.

There is more to life than increasing its speed.

Gandhi

Meditation

Life tends to speed up each and every day that passes. The most current objective adopted by society appears to be getting things done as expeditiously as possible and then moving on to the next monotonous, meaningless task. We run around doing, and doing, and doing. Life is more than merely getting things done as fast as possible, and checking items off of your inexhaustible 'to do' list. Embrace and honor the precious nature of your life today, and eliminate society's need for speed in your life.

Real Life Application

Make a commitment to break out of the robotic and unconscious path that you have been following in your life, and remain mindful and present during all of your activities. Be spontaneous, let go, have fun and, above all, be your true self. Just be *you*. It is not necessary to make a life long commitment to do this; simply do it for half an hour a day at first, and then consistently increase the amount of time that you spend on this exercise each day. Eventually, it will become part of your routine existence, and you will finally know what it is to live authentically.

Great trouble comes from not knowing what is enough.
Great conflict arises from wanting too much.
When we know when enough is enough
there will always be enough.

Tao Te Ching

Meditation

Stop your mind from rambling right now, and focus on the fulfillment that exists in every aspect of your life. It is the natural state of the Universe to provide everything you need in abundance; unfortunately, many of us never experience this priceless offering. Take time to embrace the blessings that surround you. Right here, right now, in this very moment, exists all that is necessary for you to be at peace and genuinely content with life. Immerse yourself in the most glorious of moments, the one you are in right now, and enter the warm soothing flow of the Universal Energy.

Real Life Application

Take a moment to consider what you truly desire in your life. It is important that you ask your inner most being the question and bypass your selfish ego. Your ego will always answer "I want more and more. I need more and more." Quietly, listen to and absorb the answers of your soul. Does your soul want a bigger house, another car, a new watch and a better job, or does it want simplicity, peace, tranquility, genuine love, purpose, meaning, compassion, and much more? Within you lies the capacity to possess all of the authentic desires the soul possesses; however, you must first choose between pursuing what the ego demands, or granting the wishes of the soul.

God has no religion.
Gandhi

Meditation

Religion is an aspect of life that is interpreted and managed by the mortal being. Religion has boundaries; it is exclusive, it punishes, it judges, and it ultimately has the potential to separate us from the consciousness that connects everything within the Universe. In reality, there is no religion—there is only one Universal soul that we are all a part of. Connect now, and unite with the oneness that is all of creation.

Real Life Application

Religion offers fellowship, comfort, structure, and many other qualities that are important and helpful in daily living. However, each specific religion is interpreted and perceived as 'the only way' by its followers, which is certainly a false view to hold, and can actually be harmful. Religion also contains an aspect of exclusivity; it fosters an 'us versus them' philosophy, which separates and disconnects human beings from the underlying oneness of the Universe. Whether you are part of a structured religion or not, always keep in mind that there are many paths that lead to God, enlightenment and freedom. Be sure not to follow a doctrine or dogma so rigidly that you forget the vital aspects of humanity. No matter what group, church, temple, synagogue, mosque, or other entity that you align yourself to worship with, the fact remains that we are all connected to each other.

Great is the man who does not lose his child mind.

Buddha

Meditation

Gaze into the wondrous eyes of a child and you will experience nothing less than pure bliss. The wonder and innocence of the liberated mind is most often found in the children of the Universe. Living with the same excitement and curiosity as would a child, during each moment of your life, is the only way to truly live. To see everything around you as new and refreshing is to embrace the precious nature of life.

Real Life Application

Contemplate the profound miracles and mysteries of life. Think about the process a human being experiences from conception to birth to maturity. From the sperm and egg, to the profound growth inside the mother, to the miracle of birth, infancy, childhood, and beyond. Such a miraculous process that we so often take for granted. Visualize the life of a flower from a single seed, to a beautiful blossoming work of divine art. Remember to look at life as an innocent child and you will not neglect to see a single miracle.

In thinking, keep to the simple.
In conflict, be fair and generous.
In governing, don't try to control.
In work, do what you enjoy.

Lao Tzu

Meditation

This wisdom, so succinctly expressed by Lao Tzu, is the complete opposite of the strategy that the majority of human beings employ in their daily lives. Why is that? This is simply because we live through the ego, rather than living according to the principles that are the essence of our soul. This faulty illusion that shadows our soul must be transcended. There are two choices for you to consider: follow the path of your ego, or travel the way of wisdom that is imprinted within the DNA of your being.

Real Life Application

Evaluate your life in terms of the wisdom of Lao Tzu, as expressed above. When thinking, do you think with clarity and simplicity or do you obsess and create turbulence in your mind? Do you practice fairness and unconditional generosity for all beings you come into contact with, or are you harshly judgmental and selfish? Do you attempt to control people and situations that are part of your life or can you surrender to the harmony of nature and practice patience? And finally, are you following the inner passion and purpose that you were born with or are you stuck in an unconscious and tedious routine? Answer these questions with sincerity and honesty, and decide if you wish to continue on your current path or if you would like to be the creator of a more blissful and ecstatic existence.

Laughter relaxes and relaxation is spiritual.

Bhagawan Shree Rajneesh

Meditation

Pure spirituality consists of blissful ecstasy and exhilarating soul-felt laughter. The spiritual life is never boring, stagnant or dull; it is spontaneous and filled with adventure. It overflows with feelings of joy and amazement. Enter the spiritual world and leave the material world behind; your heart and soul will reward you for this decision with genuine and enduring happiness. Your thirst for endless and genuine satisfaction in life will be quenched by drinking from the luminous glass of the eternal and all loving spirit that permeates the Universe.

Real Life Application

Implement enjoyment and humor into each moment you experience during your journey of life. Learn to laugh at yourself and the challenges that are presented to you. Smile in the face of adversity and know that this is the natural state of your genuine being. Make it a habit to smile at others, and allow your internal joy to spread through all of humanity.

Be still and know.

Chogyam Trungpa

Meditation

Stillness and simply *being* creates peace and serenity, and allows the Universe to gently guide you along your precious journey. The Universal consciousness patiently awaits your departure from the chaos of the illusory world and your arrival through the Universal corridor of quietude. Align yourself with the pure source of creation and you will genuinely experience what it is to be alive.

Real Life Application

One of the most spiritual tasks in life is to discover stillness in the midst of the chaos around us. We possess this immense power. No one can force us to become involved in the chaos of society and the melodramas of daily living. You always have the capacity to tap into your inherent state of equanimity, and avoid the noise that fills your environment. Practice stillness in all of your affairs. When you are interrupted by your demanding ego, simply acknowledge the intrusion, and return to the stillness and tranquility of the Universe.

Simplicity is the most difficult of all things.

Swami Ajaya

Meditation

The path to enlightenment lies in realizing that the essence of life is simplicity and we must practice this philosophy in each precious moment we are blessed to experience. This is where bliss is discovered. Unfortunately, most human beings will question this viewpoint and continue on with the persistent intellectualization and over complication of life. This is okay too, but prior to deciding which road to travel, one must obtain experiential knowledge of both paths. To condemn any path without direct experience and observation is to live a life of ignorance. You may be condemning the very thing that will liberate you from your suffering.

Real Life Application

Dedicate one day in your life to live completely in the moment, accepting all that flows in through your daily experience. Live simply, and from your soul. Allow the all encompassing energy of the Universe to carry you in its flowing current of simplicity and bliss. Allow all thoughts and intellectualizations to come and go like the passing clouds. Live in the Now and simply be you, right here with nowhere to run and nowhere to hide. Just you and the moment, enjoying the intimacy of life.

Compassion

VIII

WITHIN THE BUDDHIST teachings, the symbol for compassion is one moon shining in the sky, while its image is reflected in one hundred bowls of water. The moon simply shines, without judgment, or expecting anything in return. Like the sun's rays that freely give life to all, the moon radiates its brilliance upon the whole of humanity. This is precisely what it means to possess compassion. Compassion in its purest form is not biased, judgmental or demanding. Within you exists a fountain of unconditional compassion that awaits its release. If there is one thing that can rescue humanity from the vicious cycle it is trapped in, this one antidote is compassion. Compassion in action is simply giving, helping, loving, caring, accepting and expressing kindness during each opportunity that you get in life. It is realizing and embracing your intimate connection to the Universe, and selflessly giving of your internal resources to the betterment of humanity. This is why we are here!

Chogyam Trungpa expresses in his book *Cutting Through Spiritual Materialism* that "Acts of compassion are eternal; they live forever shining their rays throughout the Universe." This statement exemplifies how vital it is to act with a compassion-filled heart in each moment that we live and breathe. One good deed can set in motion a process that transforms humanity. When acting in our daily lives, it is of the utmost importance to be mindful and choose the way of compassion, rather than following the selfish way of the ego. Act with the intention of unconditional love and compassion in everything you do, then you will have fulfilled your purpose here on Earth.

If you knew what I know about the power
of giving, you would not let a single meal pass
without sharing it in a single way.

Buddha

Meditation

Sharing and giving to others is the foundation of life and
the secret to personal happiness. Human beings were
created to give to the world, and it is through the act of
giving that we receive the precious gifts of serenity and
internal exhilaration. Giving to others touches our heart
and replenishes our energy each day, so that we may move
on and consistently contribute to humankind. To give is
an action of unselfish, unconditional love for humanity.
The person who gives genuinely from their heart will be
abundantly rewarded. Through helping others, we help
ourselves.

Real Life Application

Make giving a primary task in your life. Do not only think
of this as a material act, but give from your inner most
being. Complement others, smile, say hello, and simply
act in a compassionate manner. All of this is giving. Give
of yourself on a consistent basis and you will realize the
power of which Buddha speaks. To receive from others is
human, but to give is divine.

If you want happiness for an hour, take a nap.
If you want happiness for a day, go fishing.
If you want happiness for a month, get married.
If you want happiness for a year, inherit a fortune.
If you want happiness for a lifetime, help others.

Chinese proverb

Meditation

You can continue to seek external pleasures, or you can choose to experience internal ecstasy. The creation of the life you desire is founded on the basic purpose of humanity, connecting with every human being, and lending your hand and heart whenever another human being is suffering or just needs a friend. Helping others is the way of enlightenment and will help you attain genuine success. If you accomplish one thing in your lifetime, let it be the process of losing your ego-driven self and giving of your whole being to others.

Real Life Application

Begin to ponder how, in your life, you can personally contribute to humankind on a regular basis. If you are doing this already, I applaud your dedication to humanity, and challenge you to add another dimension to your compassionate work. Be creative. If you are not directly adding to the transformation of humanity, please consider this invitation: giving of yourself to others is the greatest gift you will ever receive. Helping our fellow human beings is the reason we are here. Go forth, and add your unique touch in the miraculous transformation of the Universe.

*The smallest good deed is better
than the grandest good intention.*

Japanese proverb

Meditation

We constantly intend to accomplish so many great feats
in our lives. We dream, fantasize, and conjure up in our
imagination everything we desire to achieve, and who
we wish to become. Too many human beings act in this
manner throughout their entire lives only to fall into self
pity and despair when the regret and remorse begins to
drown them, as their empty lives come to an end. Begin
acting in accordance with your intentions. Then life's
endless opportunities will open up to you and enrich even
the most monotonous of tasks.

Real Life Application

Stop merely intending to change your life and the world
around you. Begin the act of transforming your genuine
intentions into actions, and create the *you* that will change
your life, as well as the world that surrounds you. The
smallest change in your energy has the power and potential
to create the revolution of humanity. Your good deeds
carry a positive vibration that will be felt throughout the
Universe. Begin doing your soul's work now; there is no
better time. Each time you have a good intention, make it
a habit to quickly turn that intention into an action that
will impact the world.

Better than a thousand useless words
is one single word that gives peace.

Buddha

Meditation

Talking endlessly without a significant purpose has become a way of the world. We talk and don't listen; we pretend we are listening, but we are really thinking about what to say next, and when we aren't talking to others, we are talking to ourselves in a destructive and self deprecating manner. Talk less, listen more, and strive to choose kind thoughts and words in your daily conversations with yourself and others.

Real Life Application

Be mindful of what you say to yourself and others. Do you simply talk to talk, or are you making a difference when communicating with others? When engaged in inner conversations, are you speaking from your ego or are you allowing the voice of your soul to speak? We can either communicate continuously with our mind, which most of the time is senseless rambling, or we can choose to communicate through our soul, which speaks with clarity, meaning and purpose. Express yourself entirely through your soul and the truth will be discovered.

Being deeply loved by someone gives you strength;
loving someone deeply gives you courage.

Lao Tzu

Meditation
To truly and utterly give yourself to another human being can be an immense risk. However, with great risks come great rewards. To open up and share yourself completely with another human being is the greatest act of love you can possibly encounter. Your heart yearns to experience and bestow the unconditional love it was created to share and receive. Nourish your heart and your entire being will blossom like an enchanting red rose emerging along the walkway of eternity.

Real Life Application
Having the capacity to give your love unconditionally to other human beings is the greatest gift on the spiritual path. To love is to truly live. Your heart holds an infinite amount of love that is meant to be spread freely throughout humanity. Just like the luminous and loving rays the sun shines on all beings, devoid of judgment, prejudice or bias, our love was created to be radiated in the same manner. Cultivate and spread your infinite love in all directions, and its powerful vibrations will have a lasting effect on the whole of humanity.

My life is my message.

Gandhi

Meditation

Does your life speak of a specific meaning or purpose? Or are you wandering along in life, aimlessly seeking maximum sensory pleasure through fleeting objects of your ego's desire? Success is not found in things, but is uncovered by discovering our unique, personal meaning and purpose in life. Why live if there is no meaning behind your journey? Fortunately, each human being that is born has an innate purpose pre-programmed within the fibers of their being. Eliminate the veil that has been created by society, and embark upon the purpose that already exists within you. This is where life truly begins.

Real Life Application

What is your core spiritual mission in life? What does your life say to the world? Are you satisfied with the path you have taken, or is there a higher path within you that you wish to cultivate? Articulate the answers to these questions using a written 'Declaration of Purpose' for your life here on Earth. Write out your purpose, your life's mission, and how you will succeed in accomplishing these goals. This will act as a blueprint for your daily journey of purpose.

Neither fire nor wind, birth nor death,
can erase our good deeds.

Buddha

Meditation

Every positive action that you contribute to the Universe in your lifetime is everlasting. The energy of the compassion and love that exudes from your being flows through everything and every person eternally. Your good deeds transform humanity as a whole and provide interminable inspiration. You will always be rewarded for the 'right action' that you choose on your daily journey.

Real Life Application

During each moment of each day, look for the priceless opportunities that abound to contribute to the transformation of humanity. Within each day, there is at least one good deed waiting for your acknowledgment and action. Detach from the selfish demands of the ego and align yourself with the selfless energy of your soul. Give from the compassion and love of your being, and you will discover the ultimate purpose and meaning of your life.

If you do good you will have happiness.
If you do bad you yourself will suffer.

His Holiness the Dalai Lama

Meditation

As logical and grounded in commonsense as this statement may seem, the majority of individuals inhabiting this world do not apply the simplicity of the above quote to their daily lives. If you desire happiness, you will adhere to the right kinds of actions in your daily life; if you desire suffering and discontentment, continue to behave in a manner you know is faulty and filled with selfishness. It's as simple as that; good thoughts, beliefs and deeds will manifest growth and happiness in your life; while bad thoughts, beliefs, and deeds will manifest a continuous cycle of suffering.

Real Life Application

As you can see, there is no profound mystical secret in this philosophy. However, it is valid and extremely reliable. Cultivate kindness in your heart, mind and soul and you will live the life of your dreams with equanimity and contentment. If you allow negativity to linger within your being, you will live a life full of suffering and chaos. It really is that simple; stop looking for more and more in-depth intellectual philosophies because, when you do find them, they will not suffice either, and your search will continue incessantly.

Loving kindness to all creatures;
Compassion for all who suffer;
Sympathetic joy for all who are happy;
And equanimity, a pervading calm.

Brahma Viharas

Meditation

Love, kindness, compassion, joy and tranquility are the vital nutrients necessary for the cultivation of your soul. The soul is eternal, omnipotent and omniscient. However, your spiritual evolution depends on the nurturing and development of this precious energy that permeates your being. Live according to these profound principles and you will experience the natural bliss of being one with the soul of the Universe. You may say that this is too simple, but if you align yourself with and practice this philosophy, you will cease questioning its soundness.

Real Life Application

Venture inside of your heart and embrace the genuine emotions of love, kindness, compassion, joy and equanimity. Bathe in the peace that this gives you and then allow this powerful energy to emanate from your being, spreading across all of humanity. Visualize the rays that radiate from your heart, and allow yourself to unite with the oneness that is present within the Universe. This is your divine connection. Nurture, cleanse and cultivate this direct connection, and you will experience the enlightenment that has always been, and always will be alive within your being.

There is no need for temples,
no need for complicated philosophy.
Our own brain, our own heart is our temple:
The philosophy is Kindness.

His Holiness the Dalai Lama

Meditation
Compassion and kindness have the capacity to save the world. A simple, small act of kindness can transform humanity. So, why is it so difficult to be kind to our fellow human beings? Discover the love and kindness that pervades your being and tap into this natural state. Allow this powerful energy to emanate from your soul.

Real Life Application
Every human being that walks this Earth has within them infinite amounts of pure love and kindness, and the capacity to transform the Universe. Begin to radiate the genuine kindness that your soul contains and you will then see it reflected within others. Chisel away at the shell that society has created and allow the essence of your being to thrive. You have the option to walk around and continuously push others away with the mask your ego has created, or you can be authentic, exuding love and kindness from every pore of your being.

Anger and Resentment

IX

ANGER AND RESENTMENT are two of the most powerful and violent weapons contained within the arsenal of the ego. They cunningly wage war on our internal beings, and destroy everyone and everything in their path. They are mischievous, in that they present themselves as beneficial instruments in our life, whereas, realistically, they are not useful in any way. Anger and resentment always result in injury to the one attached to this state of being, as well as to the many individuals in their ruinous path. You may justify and rationalize their existence, but rest assured this is the harmful and devious game of the delusional ego. Do not be fooled!

Don't get me wrong, I am certainly not saying that anger and resentment are wrong or bad to feel. They are normal human emotions that we will surely experience from time to time. However, our ultimate goal is to simply observe these feelings, without judgment or attachment, thus minimizing the harm they can cause. If we allow anger to come into our being and gently depart, we won't cause devastation in our life and the lives of other human beings. Implementation of this anger-releasing process will prevent the prolonged torture of resentment, allowing you to more fully experience the joy and tranquility of each moment you are alive.

So, how do we deal with those who are angry around us? First of all, using anger to deal with anger is absolutely not the solution. This creates an exponential increase of anger, ultimately leading to aggression, rage and violence. The only effective way to handle anger is by responding with love and compassion, as discussed earlier in Section VIII. Anger is no match for the raw power of compassion in action. Live each moment working toward the elimination of the injurious effects of anger and resentment in your life, and experience the warmth and comfort that love and compassion provides.

The fire you kindle for your enemy
often burns yourself more than him.

Chinese proverb

Meditation

The inferno of anger singes the insides of the human heart and soul. Often, the useless and vicious flames are fueled for days, months, years, and even decades before they are finally extinguished. Allowing anger and resentment toward another being to devour your soul to this extent, is a waste of precious life. Do not waste one more moment of your journey on the foolish and disastrous path of anger.

Real Life Application

Why do you hold on to anger and resentment for so long? Is it productive, satisfying, healing, or does it add meaning to your life in any way? Does it give you peace, contentment, or help in your passage toward spiritual growth? The truth is that it does nothing productive for you, the situation, or your life. This destructive fire inside you sets nothing right. It is, in fact, harmful emotionally, mentally, physically and spiritually. When the sparks of anger begin to flicker within your being, immediately take action to eliminate any possible harm they may bring you.

Holding onto anger is like grasping a hot coal
with the intention of throwing it at someone else
- you are the one who gets burned.

Buddha

Meditation

Continuing to harbor anger and resentment is self-destructive and counter-productive to your personal and spiritual growth. There is no room for anger to be stored within your being. This is not to say that you shouldn't feel anger. Anger, as an emotion, is natural and quite normal for a human being to experience, but to attach yourself to this emotion, and not let go, is a faulty way to live. It will take over your being, and cast a thick cloud over the luminous energy within you. Do not burn yourself due to the ignorance of others; instead, simply allow it to gently flow through the openness and light that fills your soul.

Real Life Application

Anger is a product of the ego, and can, of course, cause major complications in all arenas of your life. Anger negatively affects your physical and mental health, and is corrosive to your spiritual being. As long as you are in touch with your ego, you will experience anger in some form. However, this doesn't mean that you have to react in an unconstructive manner or suppress this emotion. You can actually channel anger's destructive energy into energy that is productive and positive. You can release this energy in numerous ways, such as writing, painting, beginning a project related to the anger, or simply transforming the energy into motivation and determination for personal and spiritual growth. Be creative!

Those who are free of resentful thoughts surely find peace.

Buddha

Meditation

Resentment can eat away at your soul, leaving only enough room for hatred and anger to reside. The erosion of your spirit will take place if you allow this anger and hatred to linger within you for long periods of time. Resolution must be immediately pursued if you desire tranquility and contentment in your life. Do not allow this disease to overcome who you genuinely are. Free yourself from the bondage of hatred, resentment and anger. Then, and only then, will you experience the bliss and tranquility that lies at the heart of your being.

Real Life Application

Resentment is surely one of those things in life that we cannot afford to hang on to. There are, of course, countless individuals in this world who are overflowing with resentment for everyone and everything they've ever come into contact with. How do these individuals feel? Miserable, frustrated, angry, full of rage, lonely and isolated—and these are just a few of the better feelings. Resentment does nothing for your relationships, or personal situations, except haunt you for as long as you choose to hang on to it. Make a list of your resentments, and gradually work on resolution and forgiveness in these areas of your life. You deserve to experience the gift of peace, without the torture of resentment.

When someone is under the sway of anger
he or she really loses the characteristics
of a human being.

His Holiness the Dalai Lama

Meditation

Anger is potent and deceitful enough to destroy humanity.
Anger awakens all the ailments of the ego, including ir-
rationality, impetuousness, hatred, fear, and an infinite
amount of destructive energy. When angry, it is vital that
you resist attaching to this force and, instead, simply allow
it to flow through you like the waves of the sea. Anger
in constant motion will dissolve without any further
destruction, but the minute you attach yourself to it, and
allow it to multiply within your being, the devastation
begins. The anger will continue to reproduce inside you,
and deteriorate that part of you which is sacred.

Real Life Application

When anger finds you lonely and frustrated in life, be
sure to deal with it in a proficient and effective manner.
Envelope yourself with people you trust, and express what
you are thinking and feeling on the inside. Talk with your
fellow human beings so that you may exterminate this
venomous disease from inside your precious being. It is
necessary to cleanse your being each time anger attempts
to feed off of your ego. Get rid of this debris quickly, and
efficiently so you are free to travel along the path of the
spirit, without deleterious detours.

As we familiarize our minds with love and compassion,
the strength of anger will gradually decrease.

His Holiness the Dalai Lama

Meditation

Anger is a product of your overly demanding and insecure ego. It continuously demands to be seen, heard and obeyed, and when it does not get what it so strongly desires, it attempts to annihilate you from within. The inner explosion of anger is your ego's cunning way of making you suffer. Embrace and caress the love and compassion that radiates from your soul, and anger will promptly subside. Anger is no match for the potency of the loving spirit of the Universe.

Real Life Application

Nourish your soul with positive energies that contain love, kindness, compassion and benevolence. Stand guard at the gates of your being for negative thoughts, beliefs, feelings and delusions. When these unwanted visitors arrive, gently guide them away from your territory, and let them know they are not welcome back. Consistently practicing this exercise will cultivate the lush garden of your soul.

Some people are like big children,
harming others without even seeing it.
Staying angry with these fools is like being mad
at fire because it burns.

Buddha

Meditation

Acceptance, rather than resistance of and conflict with in-dividuals who possess great ignorance, is one of our most useful tools. To allow yourself to remain angry with others hinders growth and obscures the enlightenment of our beings. Strive to accept those around you who tend to trigger anger and resentment, and you will surely come to know inner peace. Just accepting 'what is' and 'who people are' is the solution to all our difficulties. When you attempt to change others and reality, peace becomes impossible to obtain.

Real Life Application

Acceptance requires being right here, right now; being one with the moment, and accepting what is, without battling against the unalterable. This is a most difficult task if you live in accordance with the belief that you control the world and other human beings. Your first task is to realize that you only have control over you, and you alone; this is the extent of your dominion. For those individuals that believe they have power over everything, acceptance is almost impossible to understand. However, the earlier you begin to apply this to your life, the more peaceful and healthy you will become.

To be wronged is nothing,
unless you continue to remember it.

Confucius

Meditation

Human beings have this incredible capacity to clearly recall every negative act that has ever been committed against them. Unfortunately, we tend to forget all the good deeds and compassionate help that we receive on a regular basis. Holding on to resentment only results in the slow decay of our spirit, and our inability to genuinely feel the true bliss and tranquility of life. Next time someone acts in a negative way toward you, give forgiveness a try for your own internal health. Do not allow any more precious moments in your life to be overshadowed by another human being's wrong-doing.

Real Life Application

Individuals in this world are made up of a superficial personality which acts as a mask, or veil, covering the true essence of their being. This covering is not real; but unfortunately, this is what most individuals in the Universe give priority to when dealing with their fellow humans. Underneath this mask is the real being, the essence of that person, or their soul. Each one of us is overflowing with love, compassion, and perfection—the personality formed by the delusions of the ego, casts a shadow over the purity that lies at the core of each human being. Next time you are wronged, tap into the wisdom of your soul and look past the personality or ego that has hurt you, and, for a change, simply see and feel the essence of that human being.

In the practice of tolerance,
one's enemy is the best teacher.

His Holiness the Dalai Lama

Meditation

Patience and tolerance are two of the key ingredients that make up a genuinely spiritual life. To possess tolerance within your heart, for all human beings, is to realize the unity of humankind. To be patient, is to allow the Universal intelligence to work its cosmic magic. After all, everything is perfect if you simply let it be; so what's your hurry? These two virtues are not easy to practice in the chaotic world we currently live in. However, it is certainly possible if you tap into the love and compassion that composes your being, and offer it to those human beings that oppose you. These so-called enemies are human and, just like you, they feel pain, they get angry, they are often controlled by their ego, and they make mistakes.

Real Life Application

Along our passage through life we are certain to be confronted with individuals who we perceive as threats and enemies. However, instead of allowing these people to have control or power over you, it is much more effective and satisfying to see them as your master teachers. They are placed in your path for a certain reason and a specific lesson. You have two options:

1. You can react to your enemy in a destructive manner

and give them what they want while causing negative con-sequences in your life.

2. You can practice patience and tolerance, and learn about yourself, and life, from your 'enemy'. The choice belongs to you. You must decide whether you desire peace and harmony or chaos and conflict.

When anger arises think of the consequences.

Bhagawan Shree Rajneesh

Meditation

Impulsively reacting out in anger, in any situation, only creates great turbulence within your inner world. It is crucial to seek guidance from the wisdom of the Universe, before acting out in anger. Your most direct link to this wisdom is your breath; breathe gently, and allow the wisdom to flow calmly into your being. Then, and only then, will you recognize that the right action is compassion rather than fury.

Real Life Application

When confronted with a situation that causes anger within you, there are a few pertinent steps to take. Initially, just notice the signs of your anger within your body and mind. Don't judge this anger, just notice it. Allow it to be there while you begin to breathe deeply and connect with the divine intelligence of the Universe. When you begin to calm down, picture your anger as a dark fog within your being, and allow it to gently flow out of you when you exhale. It may be necessary to repeat this process, but rest assured, it will prove to be much more effective than immediately reacting with rage.

Let us remain free from hatred
in the midst of people who hate.

Buddha

Meditation

To allow hatred to inhabit the sacred vessel of your being, will ultimately mean the destruction of many lives. Hatred breeds hatred, and spreads like a cancer, killing everything in its path. To battle hatred with more hate, is the most devastating action we can possibly take. Seek to emanate kindness and compassion from your heart to those who bring hatred into this world. This is the only true and correct solution.

Real Life Application

Do you possess hatred for a particular person in your life? Is this helping you to live to the best of your ability in this very moment? Is it adding to your happiness, and fulfilling your experiences in life? Well, now is the time to get rid of this debilitating ailment that infects your being. Tap into the overflowing compassion that dwells within your heart, and begin to focus this healing energy on the person you feel hatred toward. This may be difficult in the beginning, but persist with this practice and the hatred will soon disappear from your life.

Death

X

THROUGHOUT the developmental stages of life, the majority of human beings are conditioned to believe that death is 'bad'. It is the 'end', it is 'final', and it shouldn't enter our waking thoughts or be discussed with others in our everyday conversations. Most importantly, we do not want death to arrive too soon for us or the ones we love. Thus, we exist weighed down with this underlying, oppressive fear and trepidation, living a life devoid of full awareness or freedom. Our beliefs and views concerning death are extremely vital in our lives; it is important to assess the societal myths that we were fed and urged to believe throughout our lives without questioning. Without becoming conscious of these faulty views, it is impossible to gain a clear understanding of what death actually is. Death is surely not this dark moment at the end of your life, where your soul is swallowed up to never experience life again.

What exactly is death then, if it is not the most horrible moment of life, waiting to finally bury us deep within the earth as our interminable resting place? First, I invite you to take a look at the perfection of the Universe as it surrounds you. Does it make the least bit of sense that you, miraculously and almost unbelievably, developed from one cell into an extraordinary human being, much less that you consistently age until one day when you may simply be buried in the ground and depart from existence forever? Not quite. Death is many things, but it is not the end. Death is simply another moment in the infinite life of the soul. It is similar to the rest of the mysterious moments in your life; although, at the precise moment of death, you make a transition to a higher dimension of being—a dimension where you continue to evolve in your personal journey of growth and development. Unfortunately, I cannot provide you with explicit details because this is an individualized process, but I can assure you that you will be at home in this new realm of existence. As for those individuals who die around you, they do not leave you. Yes, they are gone in physical form, but that is merely a temporary vehicle for their spirit. Communication continues if you remain open to the vast channels of communication contained in the Universe. Remember, you are a part of a Universal consciousness that always remains united; thus, communication is forever possible.

Death also acts as a powerful catalyst, which has the capacity to improve our present lives in physical form. Death is a great teacher, teaching us to live fully in each moment, because we never know when our transition may come. Death gives meaning; when we act with courage and confront the reality of death, we enhance our motivation to live with a greater awareness and clarity of purpose. Finally, death gently persuades us to act now, rather than putting things off for another day. Death is inevitable and will come when it is time; your task is to live to the best of your ability, in the here and now, and when death does arrive, you will be prepared to take the next step in the eternal journey of your soul.

*When death strikes there is no difference
between the way a king dies,
leaving his kingdom behind
and the way a beggar dies,
leaving his stick behind.*

His Holiness the Dalai Lama

Meditation

We all arrive in this world and leave this physical dimension the same way. This is the Universe's statement of equality and unity among the human race. However, at some point things go wrong and we are conditioned by society to believe that we are better or worse than others based on superficial and external characteristics, such as looks, possessions, fortune and fame. We then continue our exclusive lifestyle, separating ourselves from humanity more and more each day. This is not the way we were created to be.

Real Life Application

You certainly will depart from your physical body at some point in time; this is, indeed, a fact. The ultimate question I present you with is: "What will you do for humanity and the Universe while you are living within this realm?" Will you collect possessions that are meaningless and fleeting or will you give generously of your heart and soul for the benefit of all beings? The choice is yours to make. You will inevitably die, but will you ever truly experience what it means to be vibrantly alive?

If we really face up to things,
we do not know which will come first
—tomorrow or death.

His Holiness the Dalai Lama

Meditation

Right here. Right now. This very moment, filled with the loving presence of the Universe, is all that you are truly guaranteed in this life. Tomorrow, next week, even the next moment, may never materialize. Create an exhilarating adventure right this instant; there exists no future and no past. Right now is all life is truly made of.

Real Life Application

Picture yourself plummeting into the vast ocean of existence and bathing in the soothing waters of the present moment. Become fully awake and open to the sensations of the *Now*. Right now is all you have, just this single miraculous moment. You may be called to return home at any time, so remind yourself that, "I am right here, right now. The present moment is all that exists." You may want to repeat this mantra to yourself to take full advantage of being completely in the present. This may be your last moment, so make it a special one.

Whether we go underground, or into the sea,
or into space, we will never be able to avoid death.

Buddhist saying

Meditation

Death is a crucial aspect of our human life that we often suppress until it is knocking at our door. What do you fear? If we contemplate and begin to understand the reality of death, we will certainly welcome the experience when the time comes. What is so devastating about moving on to the spiritual realm when you have finished the business you came here for?

Real Life Application

Begin to contemplate and work toward the acceptance of the inevitability of death. Recognize the reality that you will die, no matter what you do to prevent it. Once you begin to walk your path each day, embracing life and not fearing death, you will truly experience the bliss that the Universe avails you. Death is not a harsh punishment; instead, it's actually a moment of celebration for your soul, simply another step in the eternal voyage of your spirit.

When you were born, you cried
and the world rejoiced.
Live your life in such a manner
that when you die the world cries
and you rejoice.

Indian saying

Meditation

The distinction that we draw between life and death is certainly not based on truth. It's simply a product of our conditioning in this world. Life and death do not oppose each other, but are unified. Death is purely another moment or aspect of our soul's eternal journey. Embrace and welcome the opportunity to transition to another dimension of life. There is no need to fill yourself with fear or dread. The world may be sad because the physical *you* has departed. However, I urge you to enter the temple of death with an open heart, for you cannot even begin to imagine what is in store for you.

Real Life Application

Develop your plan for truly living during the remaining time of your life. Keep focused on your new *Living Plan* because this is all that exists; death is simply entering another phase of our existence. What do you plan to donate to this world when it is time to move on? What do you wish to complete before you leave? These are the existential questions to focus on. When you have written out your personalized *Living Plan*, it is then time to get to work. Remember, you don't know if you will be in this realm for decades, years, months, days, or a few more moments. Get to work on your plan now, and don't let up.

Life is but a journey, death is returning home.

Chinese proverb

Meditation

Death will come when you have thoroughly concluded your mission in this physical sphere of existence. Do not fret, do not be sad, and do not despair, you will be well prepared and the spirit world will welcome you home with immense love and compassion. Your physical form and the world you reside in is only a brief stop on the evolutionary voyage of your soul. Treasure each precious moment, because you will never have the opportunity to live it again. One more thing, leave a piece of your heart behind for the benefit of humanity.

Real Life Application

Set out to enjoy each step of your journey and give from your heart in every way possible. You are only here on Earth for a short period of time, thus you must savor all of life's experiences to the best of your abilities. Eliminate the worries, the fears, and all of the other negative energies that subtract from your enjoyment of living. Your past and future do not exist, and your journey is happening *now*, so don't waste one single second engaging in anything other than pure, open and compassionate living.

If you were going to die soon
and had only one phone call you could make,
who would you call and what would you say?
And why are you waiting?

Stephen Levine

Meditation

Right this moment, who do you need to express your unconditional affection to? Who do you need to forgive, to apologize to, or just let them know you care? Contemplate for a moment that you might die at the end of the day today. Who will you contact today and what will you say? What business have you left unfinished in your life? Remember, you are only guaranteed this moment happening right now; your illusion of immortality is merely a dream; your last breath in this body may be just around the corner.

Real Life Application

Call or visit the important people in your life. Make it a point to express your love for them as often as possible and stop taking these individuals for granted. Never wait until the future to allow the love and compassion of your heart to be manifested in the Universe. Live *now* and you will eternally be grateful and free of regret.

When the heart grieves over what it has lost,
the spirit rejoices over what it has left.

Sufi epigram

Meditation

Grief is a normal process in our lives that we must fully participate in. Grief happens when we lose anything that we have attached our being to. But our most common and intense experiences with grief involve the death of those individuals we love the most. We are not grieving their death, but grieving our loss and our belief that they are gone forever. This is not reality; it is a conditioning that we have obtained from society, much like many other deluded beliefs we have acquired and continue to hold onto throughout our lives. Death is simply another phase of being. Even though a loved one moves on, they will always be there with you if you embrace and honor the eternal connection that exists through the Universe.

Real Life Application

Reminisce and celebrate the life of a loved one that has moved on to the spiritual realm. Begin your communication with a simple letter letting your loved one know how you genuinely feel about them, what you wish you had said during your time together here on Earth, and anything else you feel you need to express. You may do this as often as you feel. You may also begin talking to them in meditation or prayer. If you sit in stillness and connect to the consciousness of the Universe, you will begin to sense your connection, and you will once again be blessed with the caring presence of your precious loved one.

If you reflect on death and impermanence
you will begin to make your life meaningful.

His Holiness the Dalai Lama

Meditation

Each second of our life is so very precious and elemental in the evolutionary process of our soul. If we begin to accept and embrace our eventual departure from the physical world, we will come to appreciate how sacred our lives actually are. There is indeed a remote possibility that you won't be around to finish this book, say the words I love you to a cherished family member, or see your children advance in their lives. This is a reality that we often conceal in the depths of our deluded ego. This armor of delusion keeps us from truly valuing each present moment as the most divine aspect we can experience in life.

Real Life Application

Escape from behind the clouds of misunderstanding and gently surrender to the eternal present in your daily life. Start living each moment of each day as if it was your last. Allow the spiritual gifts of purpose, meaning, love and compassion to be the most vital areas within your daily consciousness. Be right here, right now—just as you are—and remember the impermanence of this physical life. You will never again be blessed with a moment quite like this one.

Death is not the enemy
but instead becomes the great teacher ....

Stephen Levine

Meditation

Do not drown your being with the irrational fear of death created in the penitentiary of your mind. This activity merely deprives you of freedom and the fulfilling experience of genuine living. The occurrence of death is simply another moment to experience openly within the eternity of your soul. It is, in fact, the splendid moment when you enter the corridors of another realm of the soul's evolutionary path. To acknowledge, understand and embrace the reality of death, is to experience the purity and essence of life itself.

Real Life Application

What does death mean to you? Do you constantly fear death, or simply erase the thought from your mind as if it won't ever happen to you? Think about your views concerning death and write them down. Meditate and contemplate the specific views that you have. Are they realistic? Do they add to your life? Do they take away from your ability to be present and savor each moment? Finally, what does fearing death really do for you in your life? Begin right now to face your irrational fear of death, and initiate a new life filled with freedom, presence and exhilaration, not one filled with worry, dread, fear and disillusionment.

Today I am released from central jail forever.

Ramana Maharshi

Meditation

The quote above is an interesting example of one liberated being's perspective on death; certainly, a profound and fascinating viewpoint to sincerely ponder in your own life. Our ego incarcerates our soul with its infinite desires, attachments, judgments, and never ending pursuit of exclusivity. If you are similar to the majority of human beings walking this Earth, you too labor and struggle to polish the bars of your self-created prison, presenting a 'glistening' exterior to all of your fellow inmates. Do not wait for death to be released from this entrapment. Tap into the liberation available within your inner most being and escape from the heavy chains of the ego.

Real Life Application

To be released from the bondage of your ego, you must first recognize that you are actually being held. Do your endless desires and attachments to illusive possessions contribute to your personal freedom? Do they keep you enslaved to a life of continuous pursuit for more and more of the things that actually cause your enslavement? If you are satisfied with your current state of being, don't change a thing. On the other hand, if you seek true freedom and boundless peace to exist within your life, you must sincerely assess your surrounding prison. Make a decision to take action, so that you may escape the restrictive chains and taste the delicious freedom that awaits your presence.

Enlightenment

XI

WHEN YOU FIRST HEAR the word enlightenment, many different conceptions may enter your mind. You may think that enlightenment is reserved for saints, sages, monks, and the countless other labels attached to those who are liberated or have transcended 'normal' human living. You may perceive the enlightened state as being an extraordinary state that requires living in a cave in constant meditation; thus, you all too quickly dismiss it as an option in your spiritual quest. In fact, there are many different definitions, descriptions, and processes associated with the word 'enlightenment' throughout religious and philosophical literature. Much of this information is articulated in an intellectual, complex, and overwhelming language that tends to push the 'average' individual, someone like you and I, away from pursuing enlightenment or liberation. So, here I will express enlightenment in my terms; terms that are simple, brief, and available to every human being that walks this Earth.

Enlightenment is not something that we discover in our external search for pleasure. Material possessions, money, prestige, fame and power are not where enlightenment lives. Enlightenment has always existed within you and will eternally be a part of every human being. Realistically, each individual is and always will be enlightened or liberated; they must simply realize this and cultivate it in their daily lives. So, why don't we see it and live by it if it already exists? Well, there is a dark cloud cast over our liberated being by the delusions of the ego and the false conditioning of the world around us. Our true, infinite, enlightened being has been masked by the ego, which desires nothing more than to rob us of the perfection that we were born to be.

Under the dark shroud of our ego exists a luminous being that radiates love, compassion and peace throughout the entire Universe. This is the perfection that exists within the core of our being. We must uncover this being, and then we can bask in the warmth and tranquility of enlightenment. Enlightenment is simply being able to immerse yourself in this very moment, the one you are experiencing right now, and aligning yourself with the unity of everyone and everything that surrounds us. It's being here, now, with no attachment to the delusions of the ego. It's bathing in the present without living in the illusory past or future. It's engaging in a spontaneous adventure filled with the meaning, purpose and pure joy that is already embedded in your soul. You may have experienced these things when enjoying the miraculous beauty of a sunset, spending priceless time with your children, or immersing yourself in something you genuinely love. Yes, these are glimpses of enlightenment. These are the times when you stopped intellectualizing, complaining, criticizing, judging, and separating yourself from the world. During these particular moments, you were liberated from the self-created suffering you usually endure and you entered direct communion with the Universe. You were the Universe. The Universe was you. The rays of light suddenly illuminated your deluded being and allowed you to savor the sweetness of liberation. Fortunately, this is available to you on a permanent basis. Enlightenment is yours to keep for all time. Enlightenment is you, and you are enlightened.

*When you realize how perfect everything is
you will tilt your head and laugh at the sky.*

Buddha

Meditation

It is not very difficult to recognize the precision contained within this miraculous Universe. You simply need to open the eyes of your soul, and gaze at the natural magnificence and impeccability of your surroundings. Perfection and harmony are available abundantly at this present moment; finding perfection is purely a matter of detaching from your ego's desires and bathing in the bliss-filled ocean of your natural existence.

Real Life Application

Take an hour out of your day and look intently at every spectacular creation surrounding you in your natural environment. Look up at the sky and feel the awe inspiring perfection it contains. Feel the soothing warmth of the sun or the brisk sensation of the cool air. Look at the trees and follow their development back to a single seed; a single seed which has grown into splendid beauty. Tune into the vibration of the atmosphere and bathe in the miraculous energy from which this Universe is made. Complete this exercise without the ego, without the rational mind, and without the conditioning you have been granted by society. Simply experience the *Nowness* of this very moment. Be one with all that is around you and lose yourself in the vastness of existence. This is perfection. No desires, no attachments, no expectations. Nowhere to go, nothing to be, absolutely nothing to do. Just experience what it is to exist in the perfection of the Now.

If the light of a thousand suns
suddenly arose in the sky,
that splendor might be compared
to the radiance of the supreme spirit.

Buddha

Meditation

Human beings often block themselves from the brilliance and luminosity of the Universe's passionate energy by feeding into the ominous shadow of the deluded and vicious nature of the ego. These delusions keep us caged in the darkness and fog created by the judgmental and pessimistic mind. Open your soul to the radiant nature of the Universe and allow it to nurture your entire being.

Real Life Application

We must dive into our inner world, and honestly take a thorough inventory to discover what is blocking us from feeling the natural exuberance of the Universe. What secrets and perceived mistakes block you from living and being who you genuinely are? The ego's goal is to block the light, keeping you buried in the darkness of the past and in the fear of the future. Uncover the shadows of your being and step out into the brilliance of the present.

Liberation is not something you get.
It is your inherent nature.

Stephen Levine

Meditation

We search relentlessly for freedom and enlightenment throughout the journey of our lives. In fact, you are searching right now by perusing this book; I am searching by writing this book while your neighbors may be searching through alcohol, fame, possessions and prestige, among other things. Everything we engage in is simply a quest for meaning, purpose and peace—a spiritual mission, if you will. However, as long as you continue this search outside of your being, it will never end. You may experience moments of synthetic bliss or ecstasy through temporary sensual pleasures, but again, this will cease and your ego's pursuit will return with intensified anxiety and frustration. The cycle goes around and around for infinity. Halt this fruitless search immediately and look within to discover the extravagant fortune that inhabits your precious being.

Real Life Application

It is obvious that you have begun your internal search for liberation. If not, you wouldn't be using this book as a resource for your search. It is imperative that you continue this quest within your being on a regular basis, and eliminate as many outside attachments and distractions as possible. Simplify your life and trust in your Higher Self to show you the way to freedom. Tapping into the liberation that has always been at the core of your being is the only genuine way to escape suffering. Nothing, absolutely nothing external will ever release you from the limitations, desires and anguish that fill your ego.

To become awakened one must give up his identification
with the melodramas that surround him.

Swami Ajaya

Meditation

Our world is made up of one massive dramatic presentation created by the entangled delusions of each human being's ego. We get drawn into this motion picture of false and misleading beliefs, and never escape its devastation. Fortunately, there is a way out of this fabricated production of the human ego; the way is to follow the path of purity and the genuine reality of the soul. Our soul knows nothing but truth and tranquility. Silence the ego and enter the soul's dimension.

Real Life Application

Observe the dramas that unfold in the world around you. Just look at them as an outsider and don't allow yourself to get sucked in. In fact, it is helpful to focus on the humor and meaninglessness in these ego created dramas that take up so much of our precious time. Make a commitment to yourself to detach from the dramas that occur around you and hinder your ability to experience what truly is, rather than becoming involved in the fabrications created by your illusive mind.

*Although I showed you the means of liberation,
you must know it depends on you alone.*

Buddha

Meditation

There are many paths that lead to liberation or enlightenment. No one path is the 'right one' or 'wrong one'. However, there is one requirement: you must practice and apply the principles of your chosen path with consistency and determination. No one can do it for you. Acquiring the knowledge, reciting the literature, and all of your good intentions are useless if you do not live the principles of the path.

Real Life Application

Take responsibility for your path to enlightenment and implement one necessary practice in your daily routine. Commune with nature after a long day, meditate when you first wake in the morning, or begin to pray on a regular basis; any practice you begin in your life, and make part of a routine, will certainly guide you to where you desire to be. Put one step forward and begin to walk toward the illumination that lies hidden within your soul.

A man with outward courage dares to die.
A man with inward courage dares to live.

Lao Tzu

Meditation

Courage is a necessary and crucial virtue if you desire to travel a spiritual path in your life. Fear, pain, trials and tribulations are inevitable along your inner journey. You must become a spiritual warrior willing to go to any length to continue your path of discovering and living in the truth. Society and your ego will collaboratively create enticing strategies in order to win this battle and conquer your being. However, if you persist with undying determination and faith, your soul will prevail.

Real Life Application

When this battle is fought, it is not fought with anger and rage. The spiritual battle is one of inner courage and compassion. We must accept and love our enemies and honor the obstructions along our path to enlightenment. Commit yourself to this battle filled with compassion and love, and persist in your spiritual evolution until you manifest harmony and unity in all aspects of your life. This is victory.

Freedom is nowhere to go,
nothing to have,
and nothing to be.

Stephen Levine

Meditation

Enlightenment is achieved in a split second, at the moment when you are able to experience life completely in the Now, free from the past, future, sensory desires, and delusions. It is simply being free in the vastness of the here and now, and embracing your connection to all of humanity. Be one with the Universe without judgments, fear, worry, expectations or attachments. Transcend the separation of your ego and experience the feeling of what it is to *be*, a feeling that you share with all things that surround you. Accept everything about this moment. It really is that simple, but we love to complicate it to no end.

Real Life Application

Begin to apply this to your life slowly, but consistently. Give yourself permission to let go of the apprehensive voice of your ego and allow freedom to saturate your being. Plan nothing, buy nothing, want nothing, and be no one other than your purest self. Spontaneously float through your day with no rigid plan or direction; just *be* like the air that fills the Universe. Follow the soft whisper of your soul and bask in the liberation that it brings you. Remember— practice a little at a time, as this is quite a change from the false reality you have become accustomed to.

Move into the vast, into the infinite, and by and by,
learn to trust it. Leave yourself in the hands of life.

Bhagawan Shree Rajneesh

Meditation
There is a miraculous surge of loving energy that permeates the Universe, flowing through everyone and everything. This powerful source is perfect, acting as your
gentle and compassionate guide along your journey; the
key is surrendering to this force. Let go and allow this
spectacular energy to bathe your entire being with warmth
and compassion; this is when you will experience the bliss
and ecstasy of being a completely liberated being.

Real Life Application
Instead of laboring under the great worldly illusion of
control, throw your hands up and visualize yourself being
gently guided by the soft caring hands of the Universe's
energy source. You no longer need to be the Universal
manager. You can live now, just as you are, and allow this
omnipotent force to carry you to your sacred destination.

The Ultimate state is ever present and always now.

Adyashanti

Meditation

Being unable to realize the ultimate power and importance of the Now is the greatest defect of the human ego. It is this deficiency that keeps us stuck in the darkness of illusion. Our ego consistently and harshly leads us astray as it follows the path of the delusion of time; this path chains us to the past and the future which are never a reality. The journey of the ego offers nothing but infinite regret, despair, anxiety, and an endless craving for external and impermanent desire. The journey of the eternal present, offers nothing but pure bliss, ecstatic experience and enlightenment. Like Ram Dass says, "Be here now."

Real Life Application

Whether you like it or not, it is always now and you are always here. Whether you choose to admit this and live in the moment, is, and has always been, up to you. You can remain in the delusion of time and suffer or you can be present in the here and now, knowing peace. The 'secret' to life is not a secret. It has been suggested by many people in many ways since the beginning of time: "Live in the Now"; "Be present"; "The present is a gift"; "Today is all you have"; and so forth. The issue simply is that we hear these words and say, "Wow, that's true", and then we allow this truth to escape us, returning to the delusion of the world. Well, here it is again, the secret that is not a secret: immerse your self in the present moment and you will be free. Apply it to your life if you desire to be liberated, or choose not to and return to the cell of delusion and remain trapped.

He who knows others, is wise;
he who knows himself, is enlightened.

Lao Tzu

Meditation

The journey to know the inner self is the greatest education a human being can ever experience. Knowledge of the ultimate reality and the principles of the Universe can only be found when this profound passage is initiated. You can continue to ride the cycle of suffering, seeking answers from others and the external world, or you can embark upon the vital task of self discovery and the search for freedom within. You must unveil the delusion that inhabits your being and align yourself with the truth that lives at the core of your heart. This mission is difficult and obstacles are plentiful, but if you embark on this voyage with sincerity and determination, liberation will be waiting.

Real Life Application

Become intimate with your soul and detach yourself from all of the chaos caused by your ego. Begin to acquaint yourself with the essence of your being and fall in love with the most important person in the Universe—*You*. When you know yourself, you will know the entire Universe because you are connected intimately to all that is. This realization of interconnectedness is what will liberate you from your suffering and give you peace.

Before departing, I leave you with one final Meditation that sums up our capacity to live successful and enlightened lives, one day at a time.

Every moment of your life is infinitely creative
and the Universe is endlessly bountiful.
Just put forth a clear enough request,
and everything your heart desires must come to you.

Gandhi

Meditation
You probably do not realize how immensely powerful you truly are. Within your being lies the infinite energy of the Universe. You have the potential to manifest your deepest dreams and heart felt desires. This enormous capability lies dormant within your being until you make a sincere decision to tap into it. This does not make you superior. It simply unites you with the energy of creation which all human beings possess, but, unfortunately, rarely employ in their lives. The Universe is you and you are the Universe. Directly align and communicate with this power, and you will become one with the love and harmony that lies at the foundation of all creation. Become the human being that you are meant to be, and allow the peace and ecstasy of the Universe to saturate every particle of your being. Be the *you* that has always been a part of your heart. This is in your power, so make the decision and enjoy the extraordinary journey.

Thank you for taking this brief excursion with me and allowing the absolute truth that lies within my soul to permeate your precious being.

Real Life Application

At this point, you have either been applying the principles contained within this book, reading the words for enjoyment or knowledge, or perhaps scanning the book so that you may return to the beginning and embark upon the transformational journey outlined within. I sincerely hope that you have been (or that you will begin) applying these sacred principles to your life. If you choose not to, I understand, it may not be your time. However, please share this book with others who may be ready to awaken to this wisdom. Most importantly, I hope that you enjoyed my spiritual contribution to humanity. Embrace and honor every step of your journey and always remember to be right here, right now, fully participating and enjoying the bliss of this very moment.

The 12 Steps Based on Eastern Wisdom

Step One
We admitted that we were bound by the illusion of ego-created pleasures and that our life was full of suffering.

Step One allows an individual to admit and recognize what is controlling their life. It is a chance for the person to become aware of the immense control that the ego has in their life and what this demanding control is causing in regard to self-created suffering. This awareness is necessary to initiate the process of internal growth and recovery from the demands of the ego.

Step Two
We came to understand and believe that the Universal consciousness, that force which pervades the cosmos and resides within our being, could restore us to our true nature and eliminate suffering.

This step allows one to tap into that which has all power—the Universal consciousness. This source allows for a connection with the pure-self and the true nature of the universe. This restores the individual's ability to think pure thoughts and take the right action to get rid of self-created suffering and negative karma.

Step Three

We made a decision to become detached from our insatiable ego and the illusory world, connecting ourselves to the pure consciousness of the Universe.

This step is about taking the initiative to search for one's true self and detach from the illusion of the ego. Once this decision has been made, the practice of meditation begins. This is a crucial step upon our journey because it gives us hope that there is something else besides the world of boundaries and limitations to live within.

Step Four

We contemplated and expressed, in written form, our desires, fears, regrets, and attachments of the ego without judgment.

This is a vital step, one which requires meditative and analytical thought about the nature of our worldly life without passing judgment on the past. We begin to realize that these actions were part of our illusion of what reality was and realize that now, through meditation and growing awareness, we do not have to act in this way again.

Step Five

We allowed ourselves to become fully aware of our egotistic attachments and delusions in an accepting manner.

This step helps us assess the past actions and current attachments of Step Four, and helps us recognize the true reality of the illusion. We now are able to let go of the past and live in the present moment with full awareness.

Step Six
We were entirely ready to let go of the delusions of the mind and surrender to the omnipresent Universal source.

This step is about letting go of the illusions of the past, and creating a commitment to surrender and practice the principles of Eastern wisdom. It is important to state our readiness for change and acknowledge it within our self, as well as the Universe around us.

Step Seven
We contemplated and gained awareness of our shortcomings without judging or condemning ourselves, instead allowing total acceptance and forgiveness of these ego created quandaries.

This step is crucial—one must accept that they are not their ego or mind. We can overcome our shortcomings and come to know our true self, which is the perfection of pure consciousness.

Step Eight
We began to nurture, practice compassion, and offer

forgiveness for ourselves and others who were harmed by our past actions.

This step focuses on relieving the feelings of guilt and regret for the past, and beginning to realize that those actions do not define the self. Also discusses the ability to eliminate suffering based on karma by right actions and right thoughts in the present moment where reality exists.

Step Nine
We directly apologized, hearts filled with compassion and sincerity, to ourselves and to those we directly and indirectly harmed.

This is an action step that allows us to explicitly offer our amends to ourselves and those we may have harmed in our past. This step, a continuation of Step Eight, allows the guilt and regret to further diminish, and eventually be released so that we may fully immerse ourselves in the present moment.

Step Ten
We continued to seek awareness of our true self and practice right thought and right action during each moment of our lives.

This step focuses on becoming aware of ourselves on a daily basis, and a new beginning as we live our lives fully and sincerely in each moment based on the true nature of reality.

Step Eleven
Sought through the practice of mindfulness and Meditation to improve our connection with the Universal consciousness.

> This step, meant to be practiced on a daily basis, will improve awareness and detachment from the ego's desires. This step will help one maintain recovery and stay focused on the illuminating truth of the Universe.

Step Twelve
Having become one with the Universal source, we continued to practice these principles in each moment of our life, acting as models for those also seeking the peace and tranquility of these steps.

> Finally, this step discusses the continuation of these steps in our moment to moment existence, as well as methods of sharing this way of life with others that inhabit this world. To share this wisdom with others is the primary goal of these 12 steps, which, in turn, benefits the individual as well as the Universe as a whole.

My hope is that through the application of these steps, at least one human being can discover the principle truth of the Universe, escaping the suffering of the ego's demands and desires.

Suggested Reading for Further Exploration

Dass, Ram (1978) *Be Here Now*. San Cristobal, NM:
Hanuman Foundation.

Dass, Ram (1990) *Journey of Awakening: A Meditator's Guidebook* (Revised Edition). New York, NY:
Bantam Books.

H.H. the Dalai Lama (1994) *The Way to Freedom: Core Teachings of Tibetan Buddhism*. New York, NY:
Harper San Francisco.

Hanh, T.N (1999) *The Miracle of Mindfulness*.
Boston, MA: Beacon Press.

Hanh, T.N (2002) *No Death, No Fear: Comforting Wisdom for Life*. New York, NY: Riverhead Books.

Hesse, H. *Siddhartha* (Many editions and translations are available.)

Hochswender, W. Martin, G. & Morino, T(2001)
The Buddha in Your Mirror: Practical Buddhism and the Search for Self. Santa Monica, CA:
Middleway Press.

Levey, J & Levey, M (1999) *Simple Meditation and Relaxation*. Berkeley, CA: Conari Press.

Levine, S. & Levine, O (1982) *Who Dies?: An Investigation of Conscious Living and Conscious Dying*. New York, NY: Anchor Books.

Levine, Stephen (1979) *A Gradual Awakening*.
New York, NY: Anchor Books.

Shearer, A. (1982) *The Yoga Sutras of Patanjali*.
New York, NY: Bell Tower.

The Bhagavad Gita (Many editions and translations
  are available.)
The Dhammapada (Many editions and translations
  are available.)
Trungpa, C. (1973) *Cutting Through Spiritual
  Materialism.* Boulder, CO: Shambhala Publications.
Tzu, Lao. *Tao Te Ching* (Many editions and translations
  are available.)